DAISY PETALS
and **MUSHROOM
CLOUDS**

DAISY PETALS
and MUSHROOM
CLOUDS

LBJ,
Barry Goldwater,
and the Ad
That Changed
American Politics

ROBERT MANN

Louisiana State University Press
Baton Rouge

Published by Louisiana State University Press
Copyright © 2011 by Robert Mann
All rights reserved
Manufactured in the United States of America
First printing

Designer: Laura Roubique Gleason
Typefaces: Whitman, text; Helvetica Neue, display
Printer: McNaughton & Gunn
Binder: Acme Bookbinding

Library of Congress Cataloging-in-Publication Data

Mann, Robert, 1958–
    Daisy petals and mushroom clouds : LBJ, Barry Goldwater, and the
ad that changed American politics / Robert Mann.
        p. cm.
    Includes bibliographical references and index.
    ISBN 978-0-8071-4293-6 (cloth : alk. paper) — ISBN 978-0-8071-4295-0 (pdf) —
ISBN 978-0-8071-4296-7 (epub) — ISBN 978-0-8071-4297-4 (mobi)
    1. Presidents—United States—Election—1964. 2. Advertising, Political—United
States—History—20th century. 3. Johnson, Lyndon B. (Lyndon Baines),
1908–1973. 4. Goldwater, Barry M. (Barry Morris), 1909–1998. I. Title.
    E850.M28 2011
    324.7′30973—dc22
                            2011016093

In memory of Senator Russell B. Long

The truth
seems to be that propaganda
on its own cannot force its way into unwilling
minds; neither can it inculcate something wholly new; nor can
it keep people persuaded once they have ceased to believe. It
penetrates only into minds already open, and rather than instill
opinion it articulates and justifies opinions already present in the
minds of its recipients. The gifted propagandist brings to a boil
ideas and passions already simmering in the minds
of his hearers. He echoes their
innermost
feelings. Where
opinion is not coerced,
people can be
made to believe
only in what they
already "know."

—Eric Hoffer, *The True Believer: Thoughts on
the Nature of Mass Movements*

CONTENTS

Photographs follow page 46.

FOREWORD

After November 22, 1963, the outcome of the next U.S. presidential election was, most historians agree, a foregone conclusion. Americans still mourning the violent loss of their charismatic young leader, John F. Kennedy, were not about to depose the man who had succeeded him. But incumbent Democrat Lyndon Baines Johnson desired something more than a mere victory in 1964—he wanted a historic mandate to make the presidency his own. The Johnson campaign's decision to select an innovative, boundary-testing advertising agency to help achieve this landslide transformed American politics.

Today, the 1964 election is remembered, if at all, for a single sixty-second campaign spot featuring an innocent little girl, picking petals from a daisy, who is then engulfed by a mushroom cloud. The message was that a vote for Johnson's unnamed opponent was a vote for nuclear annihilation. It was the first ad aired in the general election, and it generated a lot of attention, though not as much attention as some historians might lead you to believe. Over time, however, the Daisy spot's legend has grown, and its brand on the 1964 election is now permanent and overpowering. Indeed, whenever a documentary on the 1960s is produced, the race between President Johnson and the Republican nominee, Arizona senator Barry M. Goldwater, is usually reduced to an excerpt from this commercial.

But the campaign was about more than just a little girl, some daisies, and a nuclear explosion. The Daisy spot was simply the most powerful symbol of a new era of politics. Whether Johnson's people knew it or not, the choice to use the New York advertising agency of Doyle Dane Bernbach (DDB) ushered in the modern age of the presidential campaign. The year 1964 witnessed the fusion of political strategy and political advertising, and every subsequent race has relied on essentially the same model. In partnership with Democratic strategists and using Goldwater's own words, DDB executed crippling blows to the Republican candidate's standing. The advertising served as a crucial vehicle for reinforcing the public perception that the senator was unfit for national office.

The influence of DDB's pioneering efforts from 1964 is still very much in evidence. Hillary Clinton's "3 A.M. Call" from the 2008 primary season, for example, can be directly traced back to DDB's "Telephone Hotline" spot from its work for Lyndon Johnson. And there have been too many Daisy ad "tributes" to count.

For this book, journalist and historian Robert Mann has corralled an unprecedented wealth of archival materials and fresh interviews to provide a comprehensive picture of the often-dismissed election of 1964. He has organized the essential facts of the campaign into a concise work that is overwhelmingly persuasive in all of its conclusions. Best of all, Mann has captured the urgency and concern of what many people at the time considered to be a life-and-death vote. As hard as it may be to fathom now, the possibility of a Goldwater presidency was seen as a genuine risk to the planet at the time.

To put the stakes of the 1964 contest into a more easily understood contemporary perspective, it is necessary to consider what might happen if former Alaska governor and 2008 Republican vice presidential nominee Sarah Palin—or someone like her—captured the GOP nomination for the presidency. If you think this is an outlandish scenario, don't forget that it was the same kind of narrow movement support that Palin enjoys now that allowed Goldwater to stage a stunning upset over eastern establishment Republicans in 1964. Just as a majority of Americans took the prospect of an improbable Goldwater victory seriously in 1964, voters would no doubt express similar anxiety over a potential Palin residency in the White House. The advertising strategy employed by the Democrats against Palin would likely bear more than a passing resemblance to the techniques used by DDB to highlight the danger and unpredictability of Goldwater. There might even be another Daisy ad.

The Johnson-Goldwater matchup has, of course, been written about many times before—often by campaign or administration insiders with not-so-hidden agendas. Such is not the case here. Mann brings to his book a refreshingly objective approach along with the aforementioned surplus of research and original reporting. If Theodore H. White's *The Making of the President, 1964* was the first, somewhat biased, draft of the history of this contest, Mann's work may very well be the last and the most fair. The foregoing statement may sound like hyperbole, but as someone who has studied and written about the 1964 election over a number of years, I can assure you that it is not.

The facts Mann has derived from contemporaneous media coverage, historical government documents, polling data, and current interviews are nothing short of breathtaking. But it is his distillation and presentation of this mountain of evidence into a focused narrative that are the real achievement. For every conclusion that the author makes and for every insight he offers, there is detailed, cited support. However, what you are about to read is not just a dry recitation of facts. As a journalist, Robert Mann knows what is of compelling interest to readers: the hot and cold moods of LBJ, the flailing of Goldwater, the clever strategizing (including surprising accounts of instances where Johnson's advisers knew when to exercise restraint), the creative intensity and occasional frustrations of the DDB team, the media treatment of the candidates, and, most important, the legacy of the campaign. Every angle, including the enduring debate over the true authorship of the Daisy ad, is woven into the pages of this compact book.

Be prepared to hear a lot more about 1964 from the columnists and pundits if former governor Palin or one of her protégés succeeds in reproducing the Goldwater lightning of that long-ago election season. The more ambitious commentators will be reading this book to inform their wise pronouncements.

Bill Geerhart

ACKNOWLEDGMENTS

Many colleagues, friends, and acquaintances helped me immensely with the research and writing of this book. I am grateful to Alisa Plant of LSU Press, who is not only a superb editor but also a good friend. Alisa expressed her enthusiasm for this project from the moment I mentioned it. Her support and her determination to see it published never wavered. Along with director MaryKatherine Callaway and assistant director Laura Gleason, Alisa and her colleagues at LSU Press—a national and state treasure—have performed their jobs with great fortitude and no small amount of resourcefulness during dire economic times. Julia Smith, who copyedited the manuscript for LSU Press, did so with a keen and thorough eye.

My former dean, now the provost at LSU, John Maxwell Hamilton, encouraged me to work on this book while he and I were in the midst of research on another book project. Jack not only urged me to work on the book but was always eager to hear of my progress and ever ready to listen to stories about the creation of the Daisy Girl spot. Regina Lawrence and Adrienne Moore, my colleagues at the Manship School, cheerfully offered advice in the early stages of my research. Renee Pierce, also of the Manship School, was always ready to help guide me through the various computer-related and other technical challenges I encountered during my researching and writing.

The financial support of the Manship family, who endowed the chair I hold at LSU's Manship School of Mass Communication, was essential in allowing me to conduct the research on this book. I'm very grateful for the many ways that the Manship family has supported LSU, its students, and faculty.

Bill Geerhart, who produced a marvelous and captivating website about the Daisy Girl spot at CONELRAD.com, provided much of the inspiration for this book. Bill's website pointed me toward many interesting aspects of the story, and he was an ever-ready resource and a constant sounding board. Bill also read the manuscript and offered dozens of helpful suggestions that strengthened it.

Among those who read the book and helped me improve it in various ways was my LSU colleague Chris Weber and Professor John Geer of Vanderbilt University.

Several key players in the creation of the Daisy Girl spot generously helped me by providing valuable information and recollections. Those were: Bill Moyers, Lloyd Wright, Monique Luiz, Fred Corzilius, Colette Brunner, Ann Barton, and Sidney Myers. Myers, Wright, and Anton Schwartz also generously provided personal photographs for the book.

The staff of the Lyndon B. Johnson Library in Austin was as gracious and accommodating as always. I particularly appreciate the assistance of Allen Fisher, who guided me as I delved into the records of the Johnson White House and the Democratic National Committee, and Margaret Harman, who went beyond the call of duty to help locate photographs of President Johnson with the advertising executives who produced his campaign's TV spots in 1964.

Shirley V. Robson wrote her 1966 M.A. thesis at American University on the relationship between Doyle Dane Bernbach (DDB) and the Democratic National Committee (DNC) during the 1964 presidential campaign. Although the library at American University does not hold a copy of the thesis, Robson was kind enough to search for the original, which she had earlier donated to the Library of American Broadcasting at the University of Maryland. The library's curator, Chuck Howell, kindly sent me a scanned copy of the thesis just hours before he departed work for his Christmas break in December 2010. The thesis sheds new light on the tensions between DDB and the DNC over advertising strategy. I am grateful to Robson and Howell for their efforts to make it available to me.

I am also appreciative of the many staff members and students of LSU Middleton Library who helped me in all manner of ways. I am particularly grateful for the efficient staff of the LSU library's interlibrary loan division, who skillfully tracked down dozens of books and other materials from libraries all over the country.

Two undergraduate students at the Manship School, Janey Noble and Karsten Davis, also helped dig up all manner of records from the LSU library. I am grateful for their help and friendship. My dear friend Aly

Neel cheered me on throughout my work on the book. I am blessed to have her beautiful and optimistic spirit in my life.

Although he died in 2003, the late U.S. senator Russell Long remains one of the great influences of my life and career. Senator Long gave me one of the most exciting jobs of my life (his press secretary), and he opened up worlds of opportunity to me. Not least among those was his willingness to share with me the fascinating stories of his life during a two-year span in which I researched his biography. That he would entrust his story to a young former staff member, who had never written anything longer than a newspaper story, is a testament to Russell Long's generosity of spirit and his willingness to entrust great responsibility to those whom he believed had earned it—regardless of their age or experience. I dedicate this book to his memory with profound gratitude and affection.

As always, my wife Cindy supported me in countless ways, tolerating my periodic research trips and remaining in Baton Rouge to preside over our household and provide her and my share of love and attention for our children, Robert and Avery. Over more than eighteen years of marriage, she has never once complained about my absence while I was away on various research trips. She is my best friend and greatest supporter.

DAISY PETALS
and **MUSHROOM
CLOUDS**

1 THE ATOM THEME

It was more than two months before the presidential election of 1964 and less than ten days before Labor Day, the traditional start of the fall campaign season. In the Oval Office on the late morning of August 29, President Lyndon B. Johnson spoke by phone with his press secretary, George Reedy.

"We got to play that atom theme as heavy as we can," Reedy said. "I think it's a little too early right now to—"

"What theme?" Johnson asked.

"The atom theme."

"Yeah," Johnson replied, "A-T-O-M." He then added, sternly, "But *you* don't say it."[1]

As instinctive and canny as any politician in U.S. history, Johnson understood the fear and anxiety over nuclear weapons that had dominated American life for the previous fifteen years. Since the day in August 1945 when the U.S. Army Air Forces had destroyed Hiroshima, the world had lived with the very real threat of nuclear war. In the early years of the cold war, however, American officials continued to focus on beefing up the nation's conventional forces to blunt perceived Soviet military advances in Korea, Southeast Asia, Greece, and Turkey. Nuclear weapons were part of America's arsenal but not its first line of defense. Presidents Harry Truman and Dwight Eisenhower never seriously considered using nuclear weapons in Korea or Vietnam (although some of their military advisors did).

All that changed in January 1954, when Eisenhower's secretary of state, John Foster Dulles, announced a new American defense policy because "it is not sound to become permanently committed to military expenditures so vast [that] they lead to 'practical bankruptcy.'" To defend the nation more economically, Dulles revealed, the United States would rely more on "deterrent power" and less on "local defensive power." That meant greater reliance on nuclear weapons. "Local defenses must be reinforced by the further deterrent of massive retaliatory power," Dulles said. While he did not utter the words "nuclear weapons," Dulles's insistence that the United States should be "willing and able to respond vigorously at places and with means of its own choosing," left little doubt about the new weapon of choice.[2]

The Soviet threat and the fear of its burgeoning nuclear arsenal would dominate American politics for the next thirty-five years. The fear would result, among other things, in the expenditure of hundreds of billions for the U.S. defense budget. By 1964, Russia would possess a nuclear stockpile of roughly 5,000 weapons (compared to a U.S. stockpile greater than 25,000). By the mid-1980s, the Soviet stockpile would climb to 40,000. All the while, dominating the national psyche was the fear of a nuclear war that could destroy a large percentage of the U.S. and Soviet populations. President John F. Kennedy gave voice to those fears in 1962, observing that a "massive [nuclear] exchange" would be "the end, because you are talking about . . . 150 million fatalities in the first eighteen hours."[3]

Powerful images of nuclear annihilation captured the imagination— and stoked the fears—of millions of Americans, beginning in 1957 with the publication of Nevil Shute's novel *On the Beach*. Made into a motion picture in 1959, the book was the story of the destruction of virtually all life on Earth by nuclear war and the resulting fallout.

Kennedy entered the White House skeptical of relying so heavily on nuclear weapons, as opposed to more expensive, but far more flexible, conventional forces. Kennedy agreed with his friend and future Joint Chiefs chairman, General Maxwell Taylor, who had written that massive retaliation "could offer our leaders only two choices, the initiation of general nuclear war or compromise and retreat."[4] Said Kennedy in July 1961, "We intend to have a wider choice than humiliation or all-out war."[5] To give U.S. leaders more latitude, Kennedy's advisors developed a new strategy. "Flexible response" relied heavily on nuclear weapons but also emphasized the gradual application of force, more reliance on conventional forces, greater airlift capacity, and new anti-guerrilla efforts. (Flexible as it purported to be, the new military strategy would prove inadequate to deal with a nuclear confrontation with Cuba in 1963.)[6]

At the same time, Kennedy tried to prepare the nation for the possibility of nuclear war with the Soviets and the need for an aggressive national civil defense program, proposing $207 million for fallout shelters.[7] Such structures, designed to shield a family or a larger group from the force of a nearby nuclear blast, as well as the subsequent atmospheric fallout, were becoming more common in the darkening days of the cold war. The federal government's civil defense agency estimated that more than a million families had constructed fallout shelters by the end of 1960.[8]

In his May 25, 1961, State of the Union Address to Congress, Kennedy made clear, however, that bomb shelters provided scant protection from nuclear attack. "We will deter an enemy from making a nuclear attack only if our retaliatory power is so strong and so invulnerable that he knows he would be destroyed by our response," he declared. "If we have that strength, civil defense is not needed to deter an attack. If we should ever lack it, civil defense would not be an adequate substitute."[9]

Fears about the health effects of nuclear fallout, which had steadily grown since the first U.S. test of a hydrogen bomb in 1952, led several organizations to call for a ban on nuclear testing. Among them was the National Committee for a Sane Nuclear Policy (SANE), which sprang to life in 1957, led by Norman Cousins, editor of the *Saturday Review*, and Clarence Pickett of the American Friends Service Committee. "We are facing a danger unlike any danger that has ever existed," SANE declared in a *New York Times* ad in November 1957. Another ad—designed by Doyle Dane Bernbach, the advertising firm that would produce Lyndon Johnson's 1964 campaign spots—showed the renowned pediatrician Benjamin Spock, with a worried expression, looking at a young girl. The ad said, "Dr. Spock Is Worried." Beginning in March 1959, *Consumer Reports* published the results of a series of investigations, revealing troublesome levels of strontium-90 in milk and other grocery products around the country. "The radioactive materials which fall out of the upper atmosphere after nuclear blasts pass through a number of physical, chemical and biological processes, some of which take years to occur," the magazine informed readers. "Every day each person in the world is exposed to and consumes some measurable debris from fallout in his food, in his drink, in the air he breathes." The campaign against nuclear tests worked, at least so far as public opinion was concerned. In 1959, 77 percent of Americans surveyed in one poll said they favored the then-temporary moratorium on nuclear testing.[10]

The fear of nuclear Armageddon culminated in the early 1960s with a series of frightening—and sometimes terrifying—confrontations with the Soviets in Berlin and Cuba. The first crisis occurred in Berlin when, following a contentious June 1961 summit in Vienna between Kennedy and Soviet leader Nikita Khrushchev, the Soviets revised their longstanding proposed treaty with East Germany to give the Soviet-satellite nation control of its borders. U.S. officials feared that the practical result of the treaty, if consummated, might be no more unfettered Western access to the portions of Berlin controlled by the United States, France, and Great Britain since the end of World War II. It would also mean that the citizens of Soviet-controlled East Germany would no longer be allowed to emigrate to democratic West Berlin. Khrushchev also signaled that he no longer wanted to negotiate a nuclear test ban treaty, which Kennedy had advocated as a path toward nuclear disarmament.

It was the potential of a crisis in West Berlin—a Western enclave more than one hundred miles inside Soviet-controlled East Germany—that was most urgent to Kennedy and his advisors. Alarmed and embarrassed by the exodus of 3.5 million East Germans who had fled to the far-more-prosperous West Berlin by the summer of 1961, Khrushchev wanted to staunch the bleeding. "Berlin was turning out to be a gigantic hole in the Iron Curtain," former secretary of state Henry Kissinger later observed. "If the trend continued, East Germany, a self-proclaimed 'worker's paradise,' would not have any workers left."[11] From the U.S. perspective, closing Western routes into West Berlin conjured images of the yearlong Berlin blockade of 1948, which the U.S. and its allies overcame with a massive airlift of food and supplies. That crisis, however, occurred before the Soviets had acquired nuclear weapons. While the blockade had raised cold war tensions between the two powers, there had been no risk of nuclear confrontation. This looming crisis, however, had the potential to be much more dangerous.

Open access to West Berlin was vital to the West, as the city was not legally part of East Germany but a territory under the control of the Allied victors in World War II. "Thus our rights are clear and deep-rooted," Kennedy said in a speech on Berlin on July 25, 1961. Berlin, Kennedy believed, was "more than a link with the free world, a beacon of hope behind the Iron Curtain." It was, he declared, "the greatest testing place of Western courage and will."[12] "No one can fail to appreciate the gravity of this threat," the president said at a press conference in late June. "It involves the peace and security of the Western world."[13] In other words, the crisis over Berlin threatened to spark a nuclear war, something Kennedy clearly wanted to avoid, believing "the only alternatives were authentic negotiations or mutual annihilation."[14] As he told a reporter for the *New York Post*, "If Khrushchev wants to rub my nose in the dirt, it's all over."[15]

On August 13, when the Soviets began shutting off access from East Berlin to West Berlin with barbed wire—a division that ultimately became the Berlin Wall—U.S. officials initially worried that it might be the beginning of an inexorable escalation toward nuclear war. Eventually, they would conclude that Khrushchev's move was shrewd and not entirely confrontational. The Soviet leader simply wanted to preserve the status quo by stopping the hemorrhaging of his East German population into the West. Indeed, Soviet officials did not shut off Western access to West Berlin. There was no blockade as in 1948. At the time, however, U.S. officials were not so sure how this "crisis" would end. Therefore, Kennedy countered with a restrained military show of force, sending 1,500 additional U.S. troops to Berlin and asking Congress to increase military appropriations by $3.2 billion and to beef up the U.S. military with more than 200,000 additional troops.

Kennedy framed his request in stark terms. "We cannot and will not permit the Communists to drive us out of Berlin, either gradually for by force," he declared.[16] In a press interview, Attorney General Robert Kennedy presented a more frightening picture of the situation. "The United States and the Soviet Union are on a collision course," he said. "Unless the situation changes, we will run into one another in a short period of time. I don't think that there is any problem that even comes close to this . . . On this question really rests the future not just of the country but of the world."[17]

With tensions high over Berlin, the Soviets resumed atmospheric nuclear weapons testing in early September, in violation of their agreement with the United States to refrain while negotiating a test ban treaty. After the initial test, the Soviets announced the resumption of the "experimental explosions of nuclear weapons," which they claimed they could "lift and deliver . . . to any point on the globe." While the first test had an explosive power as great as 500,000 tons of TNT, the Soviets signaled their intent to explode far-more-powerful weapons. A furious Kennedy publicly decried the decision as "utter disregard of the desire of mankind for a decrease in the arms race" and as "a form of atomic blackmail." The chief U.S. diplomat for test ban negotiations, Arthur Dean, linked the renewed testing with the Berlin crisis, observing that the explosion was "coldly calculated" by the Soviets "in the belief that someone . . . would beg the

Soviets not to test if the United States would agree not to stand firm on its commitment in West Berlin."[18] Khrushchev, however, did not want a nuclear confrontation. He merely wanted to make a point and rattle his nuclear sabers. By mid-October, he unceremoniously dropped plans for the peace treaty with East Germany. What had appeared a crisis for the West was primarily a tragedy for the citizens of Berlin, cut off from family and friends for more than a generation.

While tensions over Berlin dissipated, Kennedy remained dedicated to continuing test ban and disarmament negotiations with the Soviets. Publicly, however, the administration signaled the Soviets that, while it was increasing conventional forces to protect West Berlin and the rest of Western Europe, it possessed a superior nuclear arsenal and was willing to fight a nuclear war. The Soviets responded with more nuclear testing, detonating a thirty-megaton nuclear bomb on October 23.[19] Seven months later, the United States would respond by resuming its own nuclear testing program.

Despite worldwide anxiety over Berlin's potential to spark a nuclear confrontation, Kennedy had never seriously believed it would come to that. "It seems particularly stupid to risk killing a million Americans over an argument about access rights on an Autobahn," Kennedy had told an aide earlier in the year. "If I'm going to threaten Russia with a nuclear war, it will have to be for much bigger and more important reasons than that."[20] Little did Kennedy know that by October of the following year, just such a crisis would bring the two nations to the brink of nuclear war.

The Berlin crisis and the April 1961 Bay of Pigs episode—in which U.S.-trained Cuban exiles disastrously botched an attempt to invade Cuba and overthrow its Communist dictator, Fidel Castro—had seriously damaged U.S.-Soviet relations, deepening further distrust and antagonism between the two nuclear powers. Nothing, however, rivaled the fear that would grip the world in October 1962 after U.S. intelligence discovered evidence that Russia was installing, in Cuba, medium-range and intermediate-range offensive nuclear missiles, some capable of reaching as far north as Canada. The Soviets were also in the process of deploying to Cuba 44,000 support troops, supported by an additional 1,300 civilian construction workers. Plans were underway for a naval base to house Soviet ships and "nuclear-missile equipped submarines."[21] Seemingly irked and threatened by the presence of seventeen U.S. intermediate-range nuclear missiles installed in Turkey earlier that year, Khrushchev wanted to find ways to counter the growing U.S. nuclear superiority. He also wanted to defend his Cuban allies who had, after all, been attacked by U.S.-sponsored rebels only the year before. Explaining his rationale for arming Cuba with nuclear missiles, the Soviet leader told associates that the missiles "have one purpose—to scare them [the United States], to restrain them . . . to give them back some of their own medicine."[22]

After a week of top-secret deliberations among his closest civilian and military advisors—some of whom argued for an attack on Cuba to take out the missiles—Kennedy went public with the news on October 22. He told the nation the United States would not tolerate the presence of offensive nuclear missiles on an island ninety miles south of Key West, Florida. "We will not prematurely or unnecessarily risk the costs of worldwide nuclear war in which even the fruits of victory would be the ashes in our mouth," Kennedy vowed. "But neither will we shrink from that risk at any time it must be faced."[23] Responding to the Soviet provocation, Kennedy imposed a naval "quarantine" on all offensive military equipment bound for Cuba, a decision that some hawkish congressional leaders regarded as weak and that others feared could spark outright war should the Soviets attempt to run the blockade.

In a private letter to Khrushchev on the day of the speech, Kennedy confessed his concern over a Soviet miscalculation, "since I have not assumed that you or any other sane man would, in this nuclear age, plunge the world into war which it is crystal clear no country could win and which could only result in catastrophic consequences to the whole world, including the aggressor." The missiles, Kennedy said, must go.[24] Kennedy's brother and closest advisor, Robert, also the U.S. attorney general, recalled thinking at the time, "Was the world on the brink of a holocaust and had we done something wrong? . . . I felt we were on the edge of a precipice and it was as if there were no way off."[25]

Khrushchev was furious over the naval blockade, which he regarded as improper meddling in Russia's relations with Cuba and a violation of international agreements regarding freedom of the seas. Angry as he was, the Soviet leader did not want to start a nuclear war. When the blockade took effect on October 24, Khrushchev ordered the Russian ships to abide by it. Two days later, in a letter to Kennedy, he proposed a way out of the crisis, suggesting that he would withdraw his missiles from Cuba if Kennedy would pledge not to invade Cuba. The next day, however, Khrushchev sent a confusing, far-more strident letter that further demanded removal of the U.S. Jupiter missiles from Turkey. Kennedy wisely responded only to the first letter, while secretly sending word to Khrushchev that he would eventually remove the missiles. Just as the crisis seemed to turn toward resolution, on October 27, the Soviets shot down a U.S. Air Force U-2 spy plane over Cuba. "We ought to go in at dawn and take out the SAM [surface-to-air missile] site," Defense Secretary Robert McNamara advised Kennedy. That advice—to escalate the crisis with an air attack on Cuba—gained support from other military advisors. As Kennedy knew, the Joint Chiefs of Staff already favored extensive air strikes against the missile sites in Cuba.[26]

Heeding his own counsel to move away from anything that would further escalate tensions and start a nuclear war, Kennedy negotiated a peaceful resolution with the Soviets. In return for removal of the Soviet missiles, Kennedy promised that he would not invade Cuba and, through his brother Robert, also told the Soviets that he would soon remove the missiles from Turkey. Khrushchev, eager for a way out of the crisis, immediately accepted Kennedy's terms. The crisis seemed averted, a profound relief to all of Kennedy's advisors, save the Joint Chiefs of Staff, who recommended air strikes and an invasion of Cuba. Fearing a Soviet trick to gain military advantage, the chiefs, led by Air Force Chief of Staff General Curtis LeMay, warned Kennedy of "diplomatic blackmail." Wise and resolute in his determination to end the crisis, Kennedy held firm. In a subsequent meeting with the Joint Chiefs, LeMay surprised Kennedy by remaining committed to launching invasion. He told Kennedy the resolution of the crisis was "the greatest defeat in our history." McNamara later remembered Kennedy as "absolutely shocked" by LeMay's advice.[27]

While the world pulled back from the brink of war, the Cuban Missile Crisis—one of the most volatile and dangerous periods of the 45-year cold war—only escalated the nuclear arms race between the two superpowers. One consequence of the crisis was to reinforce the Soviets' notion of their own strategic nuclear inferiority, especially after some in the news media portrayed the resolution as "a humiliating defeat for Soviet policy."[28] Kennedy despaired of how the Soviets might react to anything they perceived as gloating by the United States. "If we suffer a major defeat, if they suffer a major defeat," the president told reporters in late December 1962, "it may change the balance of power." Kennedy added, "It also increases possibly the chance of war." Kennedy understood that the crisis was not simply the end of a conflict but the beginning of a new phase of U.S.-Soviet relations. "Every setback," he observed, "has the seeds of its own reprisal, if the country is powerful enough."[29] The country Kennedy had in mind was clearly Russia, and its leaders worried that they had not been powerful enough—Cuba was far outside the reaches of Russian conventional military power—to control events during October 1962. They resolved that it would not happen again. "You got away with it this time," the Soviet foreign minister told an American official shortly after the crisis, "but you will never get away with it again." True to their word, the Soviets devoted themselves to vastly expanding their intercontinental ballistic missile program.[30]

The missile crisis also dramatically raised fears among Americans about the possibility that the world might soon be engulfed in nuclear conflict. An early 1963 study of public opinion in nine northeastern U.S. communities revealed that 90 percent of respondents believed that nuclear war was a possibility; 38 percent believed it was likely. Only 10 percent agreed with the statement, "It will never happen." The researchers, who published their findings in the summer 1965 edition of the *Public Opinion Quarterly,* concluded "that more than half the citizenry (at least in the nine towns) was neither blindly optimistic nor unduly fatalistic."[31]

Prior to the Cuban Missile Crisis, in March 1962, Americans had been decidedly supportive—by a 67 to 25 percent margin—of Kennedy's plan to resume atmospheric testing of nuclear weapons. By the summer of 1963, ten months after the missile crisis, public opinion on nuclear tests had shifted dramatically, as had official U.S. policy toward nuclear tests. Following the Senate's ratification in August 1963 of the limited test ban treaty, surveys showed the public overwhelmingly opposed to nuclear tests, 61 to 18 percent.[32]

These and other polls do not mean that Americans were always blithely ambivalent or sanguine about the threats of nuclear war or dangers of radioactive fallout from nuclear weapons tests. Fifty-nine percent of respondents to a national survey in July 1961 said they were very or fairly worried about "the chance of a world war breaking out" in which nuclear weapons would be used. By one measure, Americans in May 1958 were more worried about a nuclear world war than in March 1963 (75 percent in 1958 compared to 60 percent more than five years later), after the United States and Russia had retreated from the brink of nuclear war. A large majority of Americans, in surveys conducted in 1961 and 1963, told pollsters that they believed they would be in "great danger" or "some danger" of not surviving an all-out nuclear war—83 percent in September and December 1961 and 89 percent in March 1962. Asked in September 1961 about the relative dangers of their city being destroyed in a nuclear war, sizeable majorities of residents in the eastern, western, and midwestern regions of the United States believed their cities were vulnerable. As early as 1960, 71 percent of Americans surveyed in one poll said they supported passage of a law requiring every community to build a public bomb shelter.[33]

While the Berlin and Cuban crises could have sparked a nuclear war, their passing did not make Americans feel markedly safer. This uneasiness may be partially attributable to the subsequent historical, political, and journalistic commentary about the crises (particularly the missile crisis) and their aftermaths, in which some observers worried that the growth and increased technical sophistication of nuclear weaponry on both sides only increased the danger of an accident, miscalculation, or other incident that could set off a nuclear chain reaction. "We must recognize that the peace of nuclear terror cannot endure for long," Ralph E. Lapp wrote in the *Bulletin of the Atomic Scientists* in April 1963. As Lapp noted, it had been almost twenty years since a nuclear warhead had been used in war (Nagasaki in 1945), but "the tempo of the arms race has intensified greatly during the past two years," increasing the danger of nuclear war.[34]

Far more dire and frightening predictions made their way into the popular culture by virtue of books and magazine articles explaining the dangers and consequences of a nuclear war. Among them was the 1955 novel by Leigh Brackett, *The Long Tomorrow*, which portrays the United States after a nuclear war in which all major cities have been destroyed and its citizens reject all technology. Peter George's 1958 novel *Red Alert* (the basis for the 1964 movie *Dr. Strangelove* and published under the pseudonym Peter Bryant) is the story of a delusional U.S. Air Force general who launches a nuclear attack on the Soviet Union. The following year brought Pat Frank's apocalyptic novel *Alas, Babylon;* it described how the small town of Fort Repose becomes Florida's largest community after the state's major population centers perish in a Soviet nuclear attack. In his subsequent 1962 book, *How to Survive the H-Bomb . . . and Why,* Frank offered advice on building bomb shelters, the nature of nuclear fallout, the regions of the country least susceptible to Soviet nuclear threat, and how to survive in the days and months after a nuclear weapons exchange. "If you live in North America," states the opening page of the book, "there is only one certain way to survive a nuclear war: Move to Tasmania." Frank declared it "a time of personal decision. It is the time to act for peace and life instead of war and death. Every man who decides to protect himself and his family adds a stone to the rampart of our total defense and makes attack on this country less inviting. This is the moment of opportunity for the individual's imagination, energy, and ingenuity . . . Manifestly, this country is not now ready to take it, physically or psychologically. Fortunately, neither is the Soviet Union."[35]

In a more scholarly but no-less-alarming book, *Strategy for Survival*, published in 1963 by Thomas L. Martin Jr. and Donald C. Latham, the authors argued for a robust national civil defense program to protect Americans from the impact and fallout of nuclear war. In addition to disturbing diagrams of portions of the country that would be subject to nuclear fallout in a massive missile attack was the chapter devoted to "Ground Zeros," a list of the 303 American cities that would probably be targets. The Alabama cities of Birmingham and Mobile, for example, were each estimated to be targeted with nuclear warheads amounting to ten megatons, while the smaller city of Gadsden, in the same state, would "only" be targeted with a one-megaton bomb. The authors, meanwhile, estimated that Tucson, Arizona, home to a Strategic Air Command (SAC) bomber base, would likely be hit by nuclear weapons with a force of 185 megatons (the same applied to cities like Little Rock, Arkansas, and Wichita, Kansas). The authors estimated that other locations with SAC bases, such as Minot, North Dakota, Great Falls, Montana, and two towns in Missouri might be subject to massive nuclear attacks at a level approaching 1,505 megatons. Of some relief to the citizens of New York City and Philadelphia may have been the news that their cities might be subject to relatively smaller attacks of 100 and 30 megatons, respectively.[36]

These and other descriptions of targeted cities gave rise to concerns over the state of the nation's controversial civil defense preparations, which had never been given much priority until the days and months following the missile crisis. Even then, federal and state interest in the massive funding required to provide fallout shelters for 250 million Americans never gained much traction, to the consternation of some observers, including journalist Don Oberdorfer, who wrote a lengthy *Saturday Evening Post* article in March 1963. In his piece, "Survival of the Fewest," Oberdorfer reviewed what he determined as the lackluster and drastically underfunded effort to provide adequate fallout shelters, which, by his estimate, might save up to 117 million Americans from deadly radiation poisoning in the event of a massive, 20,000-megaton nuclear attack. Even with adequate shelter space, he reported, 56 million Americans would die instantly; 15 million would be unharmed or "merely sick." The five-page article featured several large photographs demonstrating the impact of a nuclear blast on a house and a full-page U.S. map, covered in long, ominous swaths of gray and black which indicated the regions of the country potentially subject to various levels of radioactive fallout. Oberdorfer concluded that, "In a curious way, the subject of survival seems to paralyze otherwise vigorous people. Partly this is because the fallout-shelter program is buffeted on all sides. Politicians are generally afraid of it, and many military men see it as undesirable competition for dollars and manpower. The optimists are sure nuclear war will never come, and the pessimists are convinced everybody would be killed anyway."[37]

Intentional or not, the journalistic and scholarly debate over the impact of a nuclear war not only persuaded many Americans that a world marred, or destroyed, by the bomb was possible, it created anxiety about the future, especially among children. "Teenagers are already old enough to be worrying about the kind of world they will inherit," *Time* observed in a January 1963 article, "The Family: Emotions and the Bomb." Quoting psychologist Sibylle Escalona of the Albert Einstein College of Medicine, the article speculated that anxiety over nuclear war might manifest itself in various disturbing behaviors:

> They ask, "Will our children be freaks?" And their doubts and fears can easily degenerate into a sense of defeat, a feeling that the battle of life has already been lost for them by their elders. When that happens, they tend to cut corners; they are lax while studying for exams, careless while driving cars. "Taking chances," says Dr. Escalona, "is what many a teen-age boy and girl would like to do in any case." They seize upon the uncertainties of life as a ready-made excuse for doing what they always wanted to do.[38]

Ten years old at the time of the Cuban Missile Crisis, D. G. Green wrote to the *Nation* in 1981 and described his feelings of hopelessness in 1963. "I remember going Christmas shopping with my mother who naturally asked what I wanted that year. I don't remember what I said, but I remember what I thought. 'What's the difference? We're not going to live till Christmas anyway.'" Green added, "periodically throughout my childhood I believed that I was never going to grow up."[39]

In the early 1960s, living with the threat of nuclear war was, for millions of Americans, a very real anxiety, only to be exacerbated by the realization, during and after the Cuban Missile Crisis, that local, state, and federal officials had never paid much attention to building bomb and fallout shelters to save those Americans who might not perish in an initial strike. The unpreparedness of civil defense officials became widely known in October 1962. During the missile crisis, citizens across the nations phoned their local civil defense offices for instructions, only to be handed pamphlets that, according to Oberdorfer, "would have been useless had an immediate attack materialized." Some cities discovered that their civil defense directors had resigned, never to be replaced. Chicago officials continued to rely on an outmoded plan that envisioned a mass evacuation of the city. Asked what citizens should do if their city was attacked, an Illinois chief civil defense official replied, "Take cover and pray." Asked what the federal government was doing to protect the nation in the event of a nuclear attack, Defense Secretary Robert McNamara replied, "Civil defense." Reporters greeted that remark with laughter. "It was hollow laughter," Oberdorfer commented. "The state of civil defense was not funny; it was preposterous."[40]

"We grew up taking cover in school drills—the first Americans generally compelled from infancy to fear not only war but the end of days," activist and social scientist Todd Gitlin later wrote. "Under the desks and crouched in the hallways, terrors were ignited, existentialists were made. Whether or not we believed that hiding under a school desk or in a hallway was really going to protect us from the furies of an atomic blast, we could never quite take for granted that the world we had been born into was destined to endure."[41]

The country's future under the threat of nuclear war sometimes appeared so bleak that one Temple University professor, writing in the journal *Social Problems* in the summer of 1963, speculated that "the search for protection against nuclear blast and fire could lead multitudes of metropolitan dwellers to move away from the cities."[42] It was a scenario not too farfetched to anyone who remembered the mass exodus of 650,000 children from London in 1940 and 1941 during the German bombing Blitz.

To a majority of Americans, nuclear war was a very real prospect that threatened the future of the United States. Wise U.S. leadership, most appeared to believe, had thus far saved the world. In the months after the Cuban Missile Crisis, Kennedy's job approval ratings soared—to 76 percent in December 1962. They remained at an impressive 70 percent in February 1963 and finally settled back to 56 percent in September 1963. On Cuba, and foreign policy in general, Kennedy's numbers were less impressive but still positive. In February 1963, 56 percent of Americans surveyed said they approved of Kennedy's handling of "the Cuba situation," compared to 27 percent who disapproved. By March 1963, Kennedy's positive numbers on Cuba had risen to 65 percent (although polling by other organizations suggested greater dissatisfaction, perhaps a consequence of the continued presence of Soviet troops in Cuba).

Perhaps the most important indicator of whether Americans believed their president possessed the skills and judgment to protect the country from a disastrous nuclear war was how they answered pollsters who asked about the Republican alternatives. In December 1962, the Gallup polling organization reported that in a matchup with potential Republican presidential candidate Nelson Rockefeller, the governor of New York, Kennedy was ahead 61 to 29 percent. The same question in March 1963 yielded a similar response—Kennedy beat Rockefeller 59 to 27 percent.[43]

By May 1962, another potential Republican candidate's name began to spark interest among media professionals and the small-but-growing faction of the Republican Party disturbed by what it regarded as the creeping internationalism of its party, which, to a large extent, was dominated by moderate-to-liberal East Coast politicians. Senator Barry Goldwater of Arizona had taunted Kennedy over Cuba the month before the missile crisis. As it became clear that the Soviets were sending troops to the Caribbean island, Goldwater urged action, not words. He scoffed at Kennedy's condemnation of the Soviet troop build-up as "humiliating" and a "do nothing policy." In November 1963, after the crisis, Goldwater charged that if Kennedy had pledged not to invade Cuba in return for the removal of Soviet nuclear missiles (which he had done), "I think it is the greatest victory Communism has won." By January 1963, Goldwater expanded and intensified his criticism of Kennedy over Cuba, this time demanding a Senate Armed Services Committee investigation into the failed April 1961 Bay of Pigs invasion.[44]

Responding to Goldwater and other Republican critics in April 1963 who advocated a tougher U.S. Cuba policy, Kennedy argued that, short of starting a war, "we have pretty much done all those things that can be done to demonstrate our hostility to the concept of a Soviet satellite in the Caribbean." In reply, Goldwater chided Kennedy for his unwillingness to go to war with the Soviets over Cuba. "The question is, are we afraid to go to war," Goldwater said in an interview with the *New York Times.* "If we are not willing to take risks in this world, we might as well give up."[45]

As Kennedy and his advisors geared up for the president's 1964 reelection campaign, they privately hoped their opponent would be Goldwater. The second-term Arizona senator was a handsome, plainspoken heir to a department store fortune who had distinguished himself as a pilot for the Army Air Force during World War II. Goldwater had gradually achieved notoriety within his party by leading the Senate Republican Campaign Committee, a post that allowed him to travel extensively throughout the country and preach his brand of ultraconservatism. In 1960, he published a best-selling book, *The Conscience of a Conservative,* that established him as the most prominent conservative in the Republican Party. At the Republican National Convention that year, Goldwater further solidified his status as a national conservative leader with an unsuccessful-but-thrilling challenge to Richard Nixon, the ultimate Republican nominee. Delegates wildly cheered his convention speech, in which he lustily attacked "the apostles of appeasement."[46]

There was, however, a less attractive side to Goldwater. A string of well-documented intemperate and bellicose statements over the years, on a variety of subjects, meant that the Republican senator would be easy to portray—and caricature—as a reckless, trigger-happy cowboy. For example, in a 1960 interview, Goldwater asserted, "The child has no right to an education. In most cases the children will get along very well without it."[47] By the fall of 1964, among other things, Goldwater would suggest ending Social Security, selling the Tennessee Valley Authority (TVA), using low-yield nuclear weapons to defoliate the forests of Vietnam, and giving North Atlantic Treaty Organization (NATO) commanders in the field authority to employ nuclear weapons without prior presidential approval.[48] Why Kennedy wanted to run against him, as opposed to the more moderate Rockefeller, was perhaps best demonstrated in May 1963 when Goldwater bragged about the accuracy of U.S. nuclear missiles, while indirectly attacking Kennedy's proposal for a manned moon mission: "I don't want to hit the moon. I want to lob one [presumably a nuclear missile] into the men's room of the Kremlin and make sure I hit it."[49]

At a press conference shortly before his November 1963 assassination, Kennedy responded to a reporter's question about Goldwater with a lighthearted but devastating comment. Goldwater, he noted, "has had a busy week selling TVA and giving permission to or suggesting that military commanders overseas be permitted to use nuclear weapons." Kennedy clearly did not regard Goldwater as a formidable opponent, telling aides that if Goldwater were the Republican nominee "all of us [will] get to bed much earlier on election night than we did in 1960." On another occasion, Kennedy joked privately, "Give me Barry. I won't even have to leave the Oval Office [to campaign]."[50] Kennedy's brother Robert remarked in a White House meeting, "Goldwater is just not very smart and he will destroy himself."[51]

Kennedy and his advisors would never know how they might have fared against the conservative and recklessly loquacious senator from Arizona. By the fall of 1963, however, Goldwater had already given the Democrats plenty of ammunition to use against him should he earn the nomination. In August of 1964, when President Johnson and George Reedy spoke of using "the atom [bomb] theme" against their Republican opponent, they were merely adopting and refining a message that Kennedy had begun developing as early as the spring of 1963. The outline of the message of Goldwater as a wild man with a trigger finger on the nuclear button was already being created. It would be left to Johnson, the Democratic National Committee, and a legendary New York advertising firm to turn that outline into a fully formed and deadly effective narrative. Time would prove them and their message as devastating and accurate as the missiles that Goldwater suggested lobbing into the Kremlin's men's room.

2 WHY NOT VICTORY?

In late 1959, Barry Goldwater skimmed the manuscript for a 127-page book, *The Conscience of a Conservative*, that had been written for him by L. Brent Bozell, an editor for the conservative *National Review*. He approved the book—proposed primarily to raise funds for a possible run at the 1960 Republican presidential nomination—with few edits. (Bozell had used, as his starting point, many of Goldwater's speeches.) While every word would soon belong to Goldwater, the book was largely Bozell's worldview projected onto the Arizona senator, a staunchly conservative man who, with Bozell's help, would soon reveal himself to the world as something of a radical.[1] It was not primarily Goldwater's attacks on big government (which must "withdraw promptly and totally from every jurisdiction reserved to the states") that placed him outside the mainstream of American political thought. It was not his argument for ending farm subsidies and price-support programs, nor his call for rejecting the forced racial integration of public schools and the federal income tax.[2] What cast him as radical was the final third of the book—a long chapter entitled "The Soviet Menace," in which he and Bozell (who was not acknowledged in the book) revealed Goldwater's views on foreign and military policy. In the chapter, Goldwater seemed to imply that a healthy aversion to a nuclear war with the Soviet Union amounted to cowardice. "A craven fear of death," he blithely declared, "is entering the American consciousness."

In the years immediately following World War II, Goldwater argued, the United States was "not only master of our own destiny; we were master of the world. With a monopoly of atomic weapons, and with a conventional military establishment superior to any in the world, America was—in relative and absolute terms—the most powerful nation the world had ever known. American freedom was as secure as at any time in our history."[3] Now, that had changed, Goldwater said, arguing that the nation's very existence was in jeopardy.

Though we are still strong physically, we are in clear and imminent danger of being overwhelmed by alien forces. We are confronted by a revolutionary world movement that possesses not only the will to dominate absolutely every square mile of the globe, but increasingly the capacity to do so: a military power that rivals our own, political warfare and propaganda skills that are superior to ours, an international fifth column that operates conspiratorially in the heart of our defenses, an ideology that imbues its adherents with a sense of historical mission; and all of these resources controlled by a ruthless despotism that brooks no deviation from the new revolutionary course.[4]

Accompanying Goldwater's conviction that communist leaders were bent on conquering the world was the belief that Americans and their leaders were not determined to win the conflict. Echoing charges made in the early 1950s by Republican senator Joseph McCarthy of Wisconsin, Goldwater claimed that traitors "and perhaps cowards" had often occupied key U.S. government positions. While stopping short of charging then-president Dwight Eisenhower and his administration with treason or surrender, he indicted "our leaders" for not having "made *victory* the goal of American policy."[5]

Making it clear that he believed in peace, Goldwater contended that such peace would only come after the United States had achieved victory over the communists, and so, before peace, might come a war. "We cannot . . . make the avoidance of a shooting war our chief objective," he said. "If we do that—if we tell ourselves that it is more important to avoid shooting than to keep our freedom—we are committed to a course that has only one terminal point: surrender." He mocked those who he said believed in "appeasement" and "would rather crawl on [their] knees to Moscow than die under an Atom bomb."[6]

Among Goldwater's ten specific prescriptions for victory over communism was his belief that the United States should not fear using nuclear weapons. Emerging in this book was an argument Goldwater would further develop in the coming years—a belief that "we should make every effort to achieve decisive superiority in small, clean nuclear weapons." That meant continuing tests of "*tactical* nuclear weapons for possible use in limited wars."[7]

Goldwater's tenth and final point was the most alarming:

We must—ourselves—be prepared to undertake military operations against vulnerable Communist regimes. Assume we have developed nuclear weapons that can be used in land warfare, and that we have equipped our European divisions accordingly. Assume also a major uprising in Eastern Europe, such as occurred in Budapest in 1956. In such a situation, we ought to present the Kremlin with an ultimatum forbidding Soviet intervention, and be prepared, if the ultimatum is rejected, to move a highly mobile task force equipped with appropriate nuclear weapons to the scene of the revolt. Our objective would be to confront the Soviet Union with superior force in the immediate vicinity of the uprising and to compel a Soviet withdrawal.[8]

Goldwater breezily dismissed the potential consequences of such a strategy—"An actual clash between American and Soviet armies would be unlikely"—arguing that the "mere threat of American action" would prompt the Soviets to yield. However, should they respond militarily to an American ultimatum, with "long-range bombers and missiles," Goldwater was prepared to launch a massive nuclear attack. "We would invite the Communist leaders to choose between total destruction of the Soviet Union, and accepting total defeat."[9]

After its publication in April 1960, Goldwater's book was an instant sensation. It sold 85,000 copies in the first month.[10] By early June, it appeared on the New York Times's best-seller list. By year's end, half a million copies would be in print.[11] While the book did not propel him to the Republican nomination, as some of his friends had hoped, it did establish Goldwater as a leading voice of the small-but-growing conservative wing of the Republican Party. It also afforded him a more prominent platform to discuss his belief about the need for a more muscular and, to some, belligerent and reckless, approach to the Soviet Union.

In May 1960, that platform was the floor of the U.S. Senate. Goldwater told his colleagues that the United States should refuse to rule out a preemptive nuclear strike against the Soviet Union. "The horrors of all-out warfare are said to be so great that no nation would consider resorting to nuclear weapons unless under direct attack by those same weapons," he said. "Now, the moment our leaders really accept this, strategic nuclear weapons will be neutralized and Communist armies will be able to launch limited war without fear of retaliation by our Strategic Air Command. I fear they are coming to accept it, and thus that a military and psychological situation is fast developing in which aggressive Communist forces will be free to maneuver under the umbrella of nuclear terror."[12]

In the months and years to come, Goldwater was not shy about expressing his views about the need to consider using nuclear weapons against the Soviet Union and his strong opposition to proposals for nuclear disarmament and ending atmospheric testing of nuclear weapons. Addressing the disarmament issue in a December 1960 issue of the *Sunday* (Portland) *Oregonian*, Goldwater asserted: "Free men do not lay down their arms when threatened by an aggressor; they feverishly produce additional arms so that they may protect themselves against the intentions of the aggressor ever being fulfilled."[13] That meant not only an escalation of the nuclear arms race but also aggressive testing of new nuclear weapons, something he had advocated in *The Conscience of a Conservative*. In the book, Goldwater scoffed at the notion of harmful radioactive effects of such testing. "The facts are," he asserted, erroneously, "that there is practically no fallout from tests conducted above the earth's atmosphere, and none at all from underground tests."[14] In late 1962, following the Cuban Missile Crisis, as President Kennedy made disarmament one of the cornerstones of his national security policy, an irate Goldwater labeled the notion "an extremely dangerous exercise in complete and total futility," believing Kennedy had been duped by Soviet propaganda.[15]

By the summer of 1963, considering a run for the White House, Goldwater would become one of the chief opponents of Senate ratification of the limited nuclear test ban treaty. The treaty, negotiated with the Soviets, banned atmospheric and underwater nuclear tests. The treaty was "sheer stupidity," Goldwater said. "Under this treaty we close the door on sure knowledge of the survivability of our second-strike capability, the very capability which, until know, has been the shield of peace in this world. We halt the search for the widest span of nuclear know-how at a point where the total test yields of the Soviet are a full third greater than our own." Before casting one of the nineteen votes against the treaty (eight other Republicans also opposed it), Goldwater told the Senate that he did not "vote against the hope of peace, but only the illusion of it. I do not vote for war, but for the strength to prevent it." Taking note that some suggested a vote against the treaty could destroy his political future, Goldwater insisted, "If it means political suicide to vote for my country and against this treaty, then I commit it gladly."[16]

By itself, Goldwater's vocal opposition to the test ban treaty would not have created in the public's mind the image of a reckless cowboy whose bravado and belligerence might start a nuclear war. Added to other reckless statements and actions, however, such an image gradually congealed. Combined with the nation's post-Berlin crisis, post-Cuban Missile Crisis anxiety, that image would prove politically deadly. Goldwater might not have cared about committing political suicide, but that is what he did, with a series of self-inflicted rhetorical and policy wounds, from 1960 until the presidential election in November 1964.

The success of *Conscience of a Conservative* led Goldwater, again assisted by Bozell's ghostwriting, to issue another book in May 1962. In *Why Not Victory? A Fresh Look at American Foreign Policy*, based largely on a foreign policy speech by Bozell, Goldwater expanded on his foreign and military policy views discussed in the previous book. The title would have been familiar to any conservative alarmed by the Soviet and Chinese expansionism of the 1950s and early 1960s. It was a famous line from General Douglas MacArthur's 1951 speech to a joint session of Congress after President Harry Truman had fired him for insubordination. MacArthur, like Goldwater, wanted an aggressive foreign and military policy that challenged the Soviet and Chinese communists instead of seeking to make peace with them. "We must recognize this war as a *war*," Goldwater wrote in the book's opening chapter. "Not a cold one, but the *Communist War*—and we must win it."[17]

As in his previous book and his subsequent public statements, Goldwater did not couch his words in soothing tones. The book prodded the reader to consider the possibilities of challenging the Soviets and to accept the near certainty that Soviet leaders would yield to U.S. threats. Citing the 1948–49 Berlin airlift, which he pointed out only preserved the status quo, Goldwater mused: "It prompts one to wonder what we might be able to do in the way of driving communism backward if, instead of merely responding defensively to their moves, we applied that power and ingenuity to offensive measures."[18] Goldwater ridiculed the "new nuclear philosophers" who believed, he wrote, "*that no matter what happens we cannot use the bomb* [emphasis Goldwater]." Should Russia conclude that such a weak philosophy was official U.S. policy, Goldwater believed, "Russia will attack; and then, in defense of our freedom and our way of life, we will definitely strike back with all the power at our command. The bombs will fall." In response, Goldwater made it clear, he would be willing to use nuclear weapons. "If we are not prepared, under any circumstances, ever to fight a nuclear war, we might just as well do as the pacifists and the collaborationists propose—dump our entire arsenal into the ocean."[19]

In many ways, Goldwater was not proposing a radical shift in American defense policy. Kennedy had often made it clear that he was prepared to wage nuclear war to defend the nation. It was Kennedy, after all, who had pledged in his inaugural address: "Let every nation know, whether it wishes us well or ill, that we shall pay any price, bear any burden, meet any hardship, support any friend, oppose any foe, to assure the survival and the success of liberty."[20] However, where Kennedy sought to resolve cold war tensions with diplomacy and the flexible application of military might, Goldwater favored military might and the brinksmanship of the early cold war years. Where Kennedy and his allies sought to reduce the chances of a military conflict between the two nuclear superpowers, Goldwater and his followers looked for opportunities to ratchet up tensions in order to test their theory that the Soviets respected only strength and, thus, would back down from all challenges.

Likewise, the centuries-old value of dying for one's country was not particularly radical. Hundreds of thousands of Americans had given their lives in the nation's defense in numerous wars and conflicts since 1776. When Goldwater spoke of war, however, he sometimes seemed to mock as weak and craven those who rightly worried about the consequences of two nations arming themselves to the teeth with nuclear weapons and as naive those who entertained the notion that diplomacy had a respectable place in U.S.-Soviet relations. Yet, while sometimes frightening, Goldwater's bold brand of military bravado and vigor appealed to many Americans. "Goldwater and his conservative message gained credence because many Americans sensed that their nation was in retreat," Goldwater biographer Robert Alan Goldberg wrote. "The new [Kennedy] administration seemed impotent while communism rooted at America's doorstep in Cuba, [was poised] to penetrate the Western Hemisphere. The Kennedy administration appeared unable or unwilling to exert military power to counter communist thrusts in Vietnam, Laos, and Berlin."[21]

As time would prove, however, one man's music is another man's dissonance. What many Americans heard when Goldwater spoke was not the gospel of sound national security policy but, rather, reckless belligerence. Like many who knew Goldwater, journalist Richard Rovere saw two sides to the Arizona senator:

> There is on the one hand, the Senator on the hustings, the agreeable man with the easy, breezy Aw Shucks Western manner who speaks in rightist platitudes but has only a loose grip on ideology and not, apparently, much interest in it. And there is, on the other hand, the dour authoritarian polemicist whose name is signed to *The Conscience of a Conservative, Why Not Victory?*, and to many hundreds of articles, columns, and press releases so heavily freighted with smarmy theology and invocations of Natural Law ('Right-to-work laws derive from Natural Law') that they have won for the Senator the warm approval of Archduke Otto of Austria, and the admiration of the ranking ideologues of the Franco regime in Spain. There is the Goldwater who can dispose of a large national problem by saying, 'If we get back to readin', writin', and 'rithmetic and an occasional little whack where it will help, then I think our educational system will take care of itself.'"[22]

As he began his campaign for the Republican presidential nomination in January 1964, Goldwater seemed ignorant of (or indifferent to) the reality that the press and the public had a far higher standard for a potential president of the United States than for a relatively junior U.S. senator. Launching his campaign for the nomination in January 1964, Goldwater seemed to stumble almost immediately. Appearing on NBC's "Meet the Press," he advocated a blockade of Cuba to force the Soviets to withdraw troops from the island and vowed, if elected, to abrogate the nuclear test ban treaty. Shortly thereafter, at his first press conference in New Hampshire, Goldwater suggested making the Social Security system "voluntary . . . If a person can provide better for himself, let him do it."[23]

Later that month, in a *Life* magazine article, Goldwater advanced a controversial nuclear weapons sharing program. "All NATO forces stationed in Europe, regardless of nationality, should be equipped with, and trained in the used of, nuclear weapons," he wrote, "particularly of the so-called battlefield or tactical variety." More alarming, Goldwater seemed to imply that he wished to give NATO allies the option of using those nuclear weapons against the Soviet Union without U.S. approval. "So long as Europeans feel that the United States can veto the defense of their homes by the most modern weapons, they will have reason to view the NATO alliance half in hope and half in fear."[24]

In late June, in an interview with the German news magazine *Der Spiegel,* Goldwater expounded on his long-held views about giving NATO commanders control of nuclear weapons. In October of the previous year, Goldwater had created a stir when he said that NATO "field commanders" ought to be given the authority to use nuclear weapons in the event of an attack. Goldwater later insisted that reporters had misquoted him; he claimed that he had not said "commanders," plural, but "commander," as in the chief commander of NATO. Semantics aside, his basic point was not in dispute. In the event of a Soviet attack on NATO troops in the field, it would take too long to obtain the president's approval for the use of "tactical" nuclear weapons, Goldwater explained. The NATO commander ought "to be able to use judgment on the use of these weapons more expeditiously than he could by telephoning the White House. They would have to have a conference on it there, and in the meantime the German air fields would be lost."[25]

Seeking to downplay the stakes involved in his proposal, Goldwater made it clear that he was talking only about "a low-yield tactical weapon." That said, he insisted that the nation "should not be afraid of war. This is brinksmanship."[26] The interview's release in early July (the *New York Times* ran a transcript of unpublished portions) sparked a debate between Goldwater and Lyndon Johnson, a debate the president and his aides relished, and one that would extend well into the general election campaign. "Loose charges on nuclear weapons," Johnson said, gravely, in mid-August, "without any shadow of justification by any candidate for any office, let alone the Presidency, are a disservice to our national security, a disservice to peace and, as for that matter, a great disservice to the entire free world."[27]

As the nation waded more deeply into the war in Vietnam, Goldwater also eagerly shared his views about how nuclear weapons could be used to assist the U.S. military. In late May, in a network television interview, Howard K. Smith of ABC News asked Goldwater how he would interdict communist supply routes running through dense jungles from North Vietnam into South Vietnam. "There have been several suggestions made," Goldwater replied. "I don't think we would use any of them." Then, inexplicably, Goldwater expounded on an intriguing option: "But defoliation of the forests by low-yield atomic weapons could well be done. When you remove the foliage, you remove the cover."[28] In his 1988 autobiography, Goldwater cited the sentence, "I don't think we would use any of them," as proof that he had not actually recommended using nuclear weapons in Vietnam.[29] That explanation makes sense only under the most generous interpretation of Goldwater's remarks. His explanation also rings hollow in light of his previous comments, dating back to 1961, speculating on the use of nuclear weapons in Southeast Asia. In November 1961, Goldwater told a group of college students in Los Angeles: "A low-yield atomic bomb might well have been used in Laos to 'defoliate the rain forests' behind which the Communists were maneuvering against the government forces." In May 1963, *Newsweek* reported this statement by Goldwater: "I'd drop a low-yield atomic bomb on the Chinese supply lines in North Vietnam, or maybe shell 'em with the Seventh Fleet."[30]

Goldwater's contention that he had not actually suggested using atomic weapons in Vietnam was further belied by an answer to Smith's followup question about whether pursuing such a course might risk war with China: "You might have to," Goldwater replied. "Either that, or we have a war dragged out and dragged out. A defensive war is never won."[31]

Their candidate's statements on nuclear weapons deeply vexed Goldwater's advisors, who knew all too well how difficult winning the election would be, even without Goldwater's troublesome statements. "When I went to bed, if ever I could have just a few hours sleep, I would lie awake asking myself at night, how do you get at the bomb issue?" Goldwater's campaign manager, Denison Kitchel, recalled. "My candidate had been branded a bomb-dropper—and I couldn't figure out how to lick it. And the advertising people, people who could sell anything, toothpaste or soap or automobiles—when it came to a political question like this, they couldn't offer anything either."[32] As the summer progressed and Goldwater drew closer to securing the nomination of his party, John F. Kennedy's prediction about Goldwater was coming true: "The trouble is," Kennedy had told journalist Ben Bradlee in May 1963, "if he's the nominee, people will start asking him questions and he's so damn quick on the trigger that he will answer them. And when he does, it will be all over."[33]

Goldwater's ostensibly extreme views on war and the control, testing, and deployment of nuclear weapons were just parts of the rhetorical puzzle that increasingly persuaded many Americans that he was not just a conservative but a radical. In June, as more moderate members of his party were working with Johnson to pass the landmark Civil Rights Act of 1964, Goldwater announced his opposition. Although he affirmed his support for civil rights in general—he had supported the weaker 1957 and 1960 civil right acts—Goldwater took exception to provisions of the 1964 legislation that guaranteed black Americans equal employment rights, as well as access to "public accommodations" (such as restaurants, hotels, transportation). "The problems of discrimination can never be cured by the laws alone," Goldwater insisted in a Senate speech on June 18. Regarding the two provisions he opposed, Goldwater asserted, "I find no constitutional basis for the exercise of Federal regulatory authority in either of these areas."[34] As *Newsweek* reported, Goldwater's position on the bill surprised no one, "but he astonished nearly everybody by the depth and harshness of his position." After his speech, liberal New York Republican Jacob Javits, who sat next to Goldwater in the Senate chamber, turned to his colleague and said, "Barry, this is a dreadful mistake. It's tragic."[35]

As Goldwater waxed on about nuclear weaponry, war in general, and civil rights, it wasn't simply Lyndon Johnson and his Democratic allies who took notice. To earn the nomination, Goldwater had to get past several more moderate Republican contenders, chief among them New York governor Nelson Rockefeller and Pennsylvania governor William Scranton. "We had to destroy Barry Goldwater as a member of the human race," a Rockefeller strategist later acknowledged.[36] To a large degree, it was the attacks of his two major opponents—aided by other Republican leaders—that indelibly secured Goldwater's image as a dangerous extremist. "Barry is on the record with statements that an opponent will use to cut his guts out," former vice president Richard Nixon said in June.[37] Just as Nixon predicted, in the fall campaign Johnson would simply dust off charges first made by Goldwater's Republican colleagues.

Rockefeller had fired the first shot at Goldwater in January during the New Hampshire primary campaign. The two men had once been close friends, but no more. "How can there be sanity," Rockefeller asked, "when he wants to give area commanders the authority to make decisions on the use of nuclear weapons?" Scranton's attacks were harsher. "What does it mean to be a conservative?" he asked rhetorically. "Does it mean you must be a trigger-happy dreamer in a world that wants from America not slogans, but sane leadership?"[38] On another occasion, Scranton asked, "[Is it] possible for us to stand with one foot in the twentieth century and the other in the nineteenth?"[39] When the campaign reached California, Rockefeller unloaded everything he had on Goldwater, branding him a dangerous radical, backed by the John Birch Society, determined to destroy the Social Security system. Worse, he said Goldwater's election would endanger the peace of the world. "Who Do You Want in the Room with the H Bomb Button?" a Rockefeller flier asked.[40]

In June, as Goldwater closed in on the nomination, even former president Dwight Eisenhower—whose domestic policies Goldwater had previously criticized as "a dime-store New Deal"—quietly maneuvered to help Scranton derail the Arizona senator, believing him too extreme to win. Eisenhower—who had earlier commented that he wanted a "responsible, forward-looking" nominee—quickly disavowed the effort, and Scranton bowed to the inevitability of Goldwater's campaign.[41]

In the end, Rockefeller never stood a chance of winning the nomination. He was a liberal at a time of conservative ascendancy within the Republican Party. Moreover, his very public divorce and subsequent remarriage essentially poisoned his candidacy from the beginning. Scranton's heart was never fully in the campaign, and Nixon was still smarting from his failed 1960 presidential campaign, compounded by his subsequent defeat for governor of California. By the time Goldwater arrived in San Francisco for the Republican National Convention in July, the nomination was his.

Successful national party conventions are usually ones in which the victor and the vanquished bury their differences and join hands—literally—for the good of the party. Such unity would prove elusive in San Francisco. Angry over the antipathy of the party's moderates and liberals, Goldwater chose a pugnacious, far-right New York congressman, William Miller, as his running mate.

Goldwater further enhanced his image as a reckless extremist with a defiant speech accepting the nomination. Inexplicably, his remarks contained this immortal line, in which he appeared to embrace the extremist brand: "I would remind you that extremism in the defense of liberty is no vice! And let me remind you also that moderation in the pursuit of justice is no virtue." Although Goldwater later explained that he meant to use *extremism* in only its best sense ("of a character or kind farthest removed from the ordinary or average"), the damage was done and likely destroyed whatever slim chance he had to win the election.[42]

The remark not only confounded neutral observers, it outraged the very Republicans Goldwater needed in his camp after the convention. Rockefeller—whom Goldwater delegates taunted and heckled when he spoke—assailed the statement as "dangerous, irresponsible and frightening." A dumbfounded Eisenhower observed that Goldwater "seem[ed] to say that the end always justifies the means," adding that "the whole American system refutes that idea and that concept." At convention's end, an aide to Republican governor George Romney of Michigan confided to a *Time* magazine reporter: "Can you imagine what would have happened if Goldwater had been in the White House during the Cuban missile crisis?" Wrote the reporter, "The aide thereupon touched a lighted cigarette to an inflated balloon. Pop!" Even before Goldwater's speech, Scranton circulated a letter, hoping to derail the nomination, charging that Goldwater had "too casually prescribed nuclear war as a solution to a troubled world. You have allowed the radical extremists to use you." As they departed San Francisco, several national Republican leaders, Romney included, signaled that they would not campaign for Goldwater. "The smell of fascism has been in the air at this convention," national columnist Drew Pearson wrote, a notion seconded by columnist Joseph Alsop, who asserted that "many Goldwater enthusiasts are genuine fanatics, like the majority of his delegates." Writing about the delegates' heckling of Rockefeller, journalist Theodore H. White later observed that the spectacle had "pressed on [television] viewers that indelible impression of savagery which no Goldwater leader or wordsmith could later erase."[43]

Despite all the anxiety about Goldwater's candidacy, there was no denying that his brand of conservatism was enormously appealing to millions of conservative Americans who wanted—in fact, longed for—a smaller, less-intrusive government. These Americans saw their federal government growing, spending more, taxing more. The culture was growing more liberal, they believed; the government, more socialist. Crime was spreading. Race riots and other unrest seemed to threaten virtually every large community. By virtue of the Civil Rights Act of 1964, their federal government now seemed to be telling them with whom they must associate or hire. In the field of foreign and military affairs, these same voters viewed with horror their nation's humiliation in Cuba at the Bay of Pigs and then, following the Cuban missile crisis, the continued presence of Russian troops just ninety miles from American soil.

In Goldwater, supporters saw a strong, assertive, plainspoken leader who would restore what many now call "traditional values." He would reverse the disgrace of Cuba and redeem the nagging shame of the inconclusive Korean War. He would, they believed, ensure that the nation's growing military presence in Vietnam ended with certain, complete victory. He would boldly confront the Soviets, not meekly negotiate with them.

This rising tide of conservative dissent (within America and the Republican Party) was not of Goldwater's making. Conservative discontent had been brewing for a generation or more, beginning with the New Deal and continuing throughout Eisenhower's presidency. To these conservatives, denied the White House for twenty years, Eisenhower's relatively moderate politics (he opposed abolishing Social Security and the repeal of labor laws and unemployment insurance) had been only a slightly more conservative version of Franklin Delano Roosevelt's and Harry Truman's. Conservatives wanted to abolish the New Deal, not simply stop its expansion. Running for reelection in 1958, Goldwater declared that he might lose, but "it will not be because [I have] broken faith with either the American people or the principles of the Republican party in this almost frenzied rush to give away the resources and freedoms of America."[44] Goldwater had not started the conservative movement, but he was rising to prominence at a time when conservatives were ready to take their party away from the East Coast establishment. Goldwater's famous assessment of the Eisenhower administration as a "dime-store New Deal" had offended Eisenhower but established the Arizona senator as a pugnacious, straight-talking conservative.[45]*

Republicans, Goldwater charged in 1960, had attacked the "welfare state, centralized government and federal control" but had actually helped enact legislation that expanded the New Deal. "We are against federal aid to schools, but we have suggested a little bit of it; we are against federal aid to depressed areas, but we have offered a plan for a little of it; we recognize that to increase the minimum wage would be inflationary and would result in unemployment but we suggest a little increase; we

*The same scholars' research of public opinion data suggested that, in the 1950s, at least, there had been no "silent pool" of frustrated conservative Republicans. Their examination of polling data indicated "that in 1952 those Republicans who reported during the campaign that they would have preferred the 'conservative' Taft over the 'liberal' Eisenhower—exactly those Republicans to whom the theory refers—actually turned out in much *higher* rates to vote for Eisenhower in the November election (94 percent) than did the set of Republicans who indicated satisfaction with Eisenhower's nomination (84 percent)" (Philip E. Converse, Aage R. Clausen, and Warren E. Miller, "Electoral Myth and Reality: The 1964 Election," *American Political Science Review* 59, no. 2 [June 1965]: 321–36).

have constantly held that the federal government should not provide so-
cialized medicine, but now a spokesman offers a plan for a little of it."[46]

The Republican liberals who abetted Eisenhower's New Deal–light
program were guilty of what some called "me-tooism." Failure to win the
White House in 1960, these conservatives believed, had not occurred because Americans rejected conservative ideology. Rather, it was because
the Republican Party's candidates were not conservative enough. Con-
cerning this theory, embraced by Goldwater and his followers, a trio of
political scientists explained in 1965 that Republican presidential candidates "tended to lose not because there was any lack of potential Republican votes (as the superficial observer might have thought), but because
many of the 'real' Republicans were sufficiently offended by 'me-tooism'
that they simply didn't bother to vote at all. Nominate a true Republican
rather than a Tweedledee, the theory went, and enough of these stay-
at-homes would return to the polls to put him into the White House."[47]

Time would prove that the disastrous 1964 Goldwater campaign—
deemed by many at the time as conservatism's last gasp—was actually
the birth pains of a conservative movement that would reach adulthood
in 1980 with the election of President Ronald Reagan. In 1964, however,
the conservative Republican troops struggled to establish not simply the
legitimacy of their ideology but the sanity of their candidate. "If you were
to direct a petition to heaven, asking angelic dispatch of the ideal candidate for the American Presidency," Goldwater's then-speechwriter, Stephen Hess, later wrote, "the odds are 100-1 that the return mail would
not bring you Barry Goldwater."[48]

Richard Rovere believed that the "real" Goldwater held more moderate views on many issues than the aides and conservative intellectuals
who wrote books and articles for him. "We tend to assume that the product of the press agents and the ghostwriters will somehow appear to be
more appealing, freer of blemishes, worthier of trust than the original,"
Rovere wrote. "Otherwise, why bother? Why tamper with nature except
to improve on it? But those who have brought the other Goldwater into
being by putting words into his mouth have produced not a better Goldwater, but, politically a far worse one."[49]

For Johnson and his running mate, Senator Hubert Humphrey of Minnesota, Goldwater's far-right ideology and bellicose rhetoric were valuable
assets, easily exploited and already expertly characterized by Goldwater's
Republican primary opponents. Privately, Johnson told associates early

in 1964 that he believed Goldwater was "nutty as a fruitcake."[50] In July, speaking to Attorney General Robert Kennedy, Johnson previewed his campaign's coming attacks on Goldwater, telling Kennedy he wanted to focus on his opponent's "impetuousness and his impulsiveness" and his reckless talk about nuclear weapons.[51] In early August, before his nomination for vice president, Humphrey—perhaps trying out for the role of Johnson's attack dog—told a group of Young Democrats in West Virginia that the American people did not want a "twitchy, nervous, emotional hand on the atomic bomb." Humphrey, whose remarks were reported in the *New York Times*, explained: "I want to be sure that whoever is President of the United States is calm and strong and resolute, and does not think with his blood."[52]

At the Democratic National Convention in Atlantic City in late August, the Johnson campaign launched what would become a sustained attack on Goldwater's credibility. Humphrey (with speechwriting assistance from Johnson aide Bill Moyers) fired up delegates with a lusty verbal assault on Goldwater. Humphrey declared that Goldwater "has been facing backward against the mainstream of American history. He is not only out of tune with the great majority of his countrymen, he is even out of step with his own party." Humphrey ridiculed Goldwater's vote against the test ban treaty, observing that "most Democrats and Republicans" supported the treaty, "but not the temporary Republican spokesman."[53]

In his convention speech, Johnson never mentioned Goldwater by name, but there was no mistaking what he meant by this statement: "There is no place in today's world for weakness. But there is also no place in today's world for recklessness. We cannot act rashly with the nuclear weapons that could destroy us all. The only course is to press with all our mind and all our will to make sure, doubly sure, that these weapons are never really used at all."[54]

In the face of what Goldwater and his advisors knew would be a brutal assault on the Republican candidate's perceived extremism, Goldwater would soon double down on his rhetoric as the fall campaign unfolded. "Of Barry Goldwater's campaign," Theodore White wrote, "it may be fairly said that no man ever began a Presidential effort more deeply wounded by his own nomination, suffering more insurmountable handicaps. And then it must be added that he made the worst of them."[55] Reviewing the campaign twenty years later for her landmark history of presidential campaign advertising, Kathleen Hall Jamieson noted that Goldwater seemed "more interested in winning the point" than the election. "Indeed, in what was one of the strangest campaigns in modern history," Jamieson wrote, "Barry Goldwater attempted, in the two short months from Labor Day to November 4, to move the vast majority of the middle to where *he* stood rather than attempting to present his philosophy in terms palatable to the moderate middle."[56] Goldwater was not about to trim his sails in order to win an election. "I was going to be my own man," he wrote later in a memoir, "not packaged for the voters by Madison Avenue and a lot of other slick professionals who made me very uncomfortable."[57]

Goldwater conveniently omitted the fact that his campaign did hire a professional advertising firm to help shape his image. The problem, however, was that Goldwater's statements and actions over the previous four years had already solidified in voters' minds a less-than-appealing image. Asked in January 1964 by the Louis Harris polling organization, only 32 percent of those surveyed agreed with Goldwater's opposition to the test ban treaty.[58] In another Harris poll in July, 72 percent said they believed— the candidate's explanations to the contrary notwithstanding—that Goldwater favored using an atomic bomb in Asia. An even larger percentage, 82 percent, said they opposed fighting in Asia with atomic weapons.[59] Of those surveyed by the Gallup organization in August 1964, only 13 percent believed that Goldwater possessed "good judgment," while more than half either described him as "reckless" or as someone with "poor judgment."[60] By September, 45 percent of those surveyed by Harris regarded him as a radical (another 40 percent would describe him as conservative).[61] Perhaps Louis Harris summed up Goldwater's position best immediately after the Republican National Convention: "Rarely had a man in such a commanding position for a major party presidential nomination found his political position[,] as understood by the public[,] to be so diametrically opposed by the voters themselves."[62]

Perhaps even better than Goldwater's campaign, Johnson's aides understood these numbers and, more important, how to exploit them. "The issue of the campaign," Johnson's speechwriter Richard Goodwin wrote, "was not the Democratic record, not liberalism, not Lyndon Johnson— but Barry Goldwater himself. It was an incumbent's dream, and a challenger's nightmare."[63] Johnson knew all that he had to do was to exploit the fear Americans already had about Goldwater and his policies.

In late August, Johnson met with his campaign team in the White

House. "Now, boys, let's hear what you have in mind for me." After about twenty minutes of discussion about various strategies, Johnson interrupted. "You fellows are the experts," he said,

> but this is how I see it. I'm the president. That's our greatest asset. And I don't want to piss it away by getting down in the mud with Barry . . . My daddy once told me about the time a fire broke out in a three-story building in Johnson City. Old Man Hutchinson was trapped on the third floor and the fire ladder was too short to reach him. So Jim Morsund, he was one of the volunteer fire chiefs, grabbed a piece of rope, tied a loop in it, threw it up to Mr. Hutchinson, and told him to tie it around his waist . . . Then he pulled him down.

"Now," Johnson concluded, "Barry's already got a rope around him, and he's knotted it pretty firm. All you have to do is give a little tug. And while he's fighting to keep standing, I'll just sit right here and run the country."[64]

3 RULES ARE MADE TO BE BROKEN

"Think Small." The slogan for the new U.S. campaign in 1960 for the German automaker Volkswagen communicated anything but a modest approach to advertising. Its creator, the emerging New York–based agency Doyle Dane Bernbach (DDB), was sparking a revolution in the advertising business with its fresh approach to selling its clients' products. DDB was not a big firm in the late 1950s (in 1959 it was nearly eightieth in total billings of its clients in the rankings of U.S. ad agencies), but its ambitions were enormous and its innovative ads were about to revolutionize the industry.

Since the 1940s, advertising had been mostly about the hard sell. "Filtered through business school models of persuasion and frequency, most of the ads being produced by Madison Avenue were static and saccharine," auto industry journalist David Kiley concluded in his history of Volkswagen in the United States. "There was no soul in advertising."[1] Most ad firms had long followed the research-based models pioneered by advertising giants like David Ogilvy, of Ogilvy and Mather, and his mentor, Rosser Reeves, head of the large Ted Bates agency. Reeves, who had influenced early political advertising with unique TV spots for Dwight Eisenhower in 1952, had revolutionized his industry by articulating the "unique selling proposition" (USP), the singular claim or feature about a product that separated it from its competitors. As described in his 1961 book, *Reality in Advertising*, the USP was "not just words, not just product puffery, not just show-window advertising. Each advertisement must say to each reader: 'Buy *this* product, and you will get *this* specific benefit.'" A believer in the "hard sell," Reeves argued that advertising was simply "a tool to convey ideas and information about a product."[2] Ogilvy, meanwhile, preached the religion of product and market research, believed in "branding by personality" (best exemplified by his firm's creation of the enormously successful eye-patch-wearing "man in the Hathaway shirt"). He frowned upon teamwork as a way to produce good advertising. "No advertisement, no commercial and no image can be created by a committee."[3]

DDB—created in 1949 and headed by Ned Doyle, Maxwell Dane, and William Bernbach—synthesized elements of Reeves's and Ogilvy's approaches, with several notable refinements. "Rules are made to be broken," Bernbach, the agency's creative genius, often told his employees. Other times he instructed them that "playing it safe can be the most dangerous thing in the world, because you're presenting people with an idea they've seen before, and you won't have an impact."[4] Bernbach decried Reeves's "hard-sell" techniques. "Just make sure your advertising is saying something with substance, something that will serve and inform the consumer, and be sure you're saying it like it's never been said before."[5] At DDB, research was decidedly not among the highest priorities. "I consider *research* the major culprit in the advertising picture," Bernbach said in 1957. "It has done more to perpetuate creative mediocrity than any other factor."[6]

"If the history of advertising has one overriding theme," Mark Tungage wrote in *Adland: A Global History of Advertising,* "it is this constant tug of war between two schools: the creatives, who believe art inspires consumers to buy; and the pragmatists, who sell based on facts and come armed with reams of research."[7] Bernbach was clearly in the former school. "Bernbach was an ideologue of disorder, an untiring propagandist for the business value of modern art," journalist Thomas Frank wrote in his history of 1960s counterculture, *The Conquest of Cool.*[8] In 1947, two years before he left Grey Advertising to form his own agency, Bernbach offered the following observations on advertising in a letter to his employers:

> There are a lot of great technicians in advertising. And unfortunately they talk the best game. They know all the rules. They can tell you that people in an ad will get you greater readership. They can tell you that a sentence should be this short or that long. They can tell you that body copy should be broken up for easier and more inviting reading. They can give you fact after fact after fact. They are the scientists of advertising. But there's one little rub. Advertising is fundamentally persuasion and persuasion happens to be not a science, but an art.[9]

The fifty-three-year-old Bernbach was balding and soft-spoken. Standing at five feet, seven inches, conservative in manner and appearance, he was not an imposing figure. He was, however, blessed with enormous ambition and a healthy ego. His looks were deceiving. He was, in fact, a powerful force who, more often than not, won arguments with colleagues and clients. Beyond his fervent belief in creative experimentation, Bernbach's most important innovation may have been his success in reimagining the structure and function of an advertising agency. "If Bernbach did not invent the creative team," journalist Stephen Fox wrote in a history of American advertising, "he refined the concept and coaxed better work from it." Prior to DDB's advent, advertising firms had generally shared Ogilvy's aversion to committees, following a linear creative process. Copywriters produced the words, which they passed along to art directors, who used the concept and the language to complete the ad. The two departments rarely collaborated. Bernbach turned that process on its head, creating teams of copywriters, art directors, and other agency staff. "Typically," an account manager once explained, "an ad [at DDB] begins with an art director and a copywriter sitting down together in a room, with or without direction from the client or the account people. Together they develop a picture-and-headline combination that seems promising."[10] Of Bernbach's method, advertising veteran Jerry Della Femina observed, "I think he got the feeling that it was easier to have two bright people sit there thinking about the same problem than to have one bright person using himself as a judge."[11] Sidney Myers, who joined the firm in 1958 and later became senior art director, regarded Bernbach as "a genius at motivating people and giving them the room to be creative. It was a place where you could reach for the sky and, if you stumbled, you wouldn't be punished for it."[12] As one DDB copywriter later observed, "He changed forever the direction of all advertising by destroying old conventions and hoary restrictions and rethinking how advertising works."[13] In presenting Bernbach a special award in 1959, the Art Directors Club cited him for "his impatience with the trite and usual, for proving that boldness and originality in art direction are successful selling tools, for working with art directors and encouraging them to grow creatively."[14] The result of the approach was a fresh, new synergy on Madison Avenue.

In time, Bernbach and his new firm would produce print ads that revolutionized the industry and won the firm scores of awards and accolades. While its groundbreaking ads for Ohrbach's department store, El Al Israel Airlines, Polaroid, Thom McAn, and Levy's Jewish-style rye bread established the firm as a creative force in the early 1950s, it was DDB's stunningly original work for Volkswagen, beginning in 1960, that caught the eye of President Kennedy as he contemplated his 1964 reelection campaign.

Mediocre, bland, and conventional, automobile advertisements were not among the best examples of advertising excellence in the late 1950s. For decades, Detroit had featured artists' illustrations of its products (rarely photographs), which, in the hands of an "artistic elongator," often exaggerated the cars' proportions. DDB's approach to Volkswagen was new and honest. The print ads typically featured a photograph of a Volkswagen Beetle or station wagon over a short, punchy, self-deprecating headline, followed by several paragraphs of text. (Ironically, this design was something of an Ogilvy trademark, used for other types of products.) The first DDB magazine ad for Volkswagen in 1960 became a symbol for the dozens that followed. It featured a small photograph of a Beetle in the upper left corner of a large white space. At the bottom, over several paragraphs of irreverent text, was the simple headline: "Think small." (Many years later, *Advertising Age* declared "Think small" the most successful advertising campaign of the twentieth century.)[15] Another ad featured an arresting, unprecedented advertising approach, especially for an automobile. Over a large photograph of a Beetle was the simple headline, "Lemon." The text, spotlighting the company's meticulous inspection program, explained, "This Volkswagen missed the boat. The chrome on the glove compartment is blemished and must be replaced. Chances are you wouldn't have noticed it; Inspector Kurt Kroner did . . . We pluck the lemons; you get the plums."[16]

The fresh, honest print ads, and the subsequent television commercials that DDB produced for the German company, were enormously popular and were part of the reason annual Volkswagen sales in the United States soared from 190,000 in 1960 to 567,000 by 1968.[17] "Prose more than copywriting," auto journalist David Kiley wrote, "the ads were different from anything else the U.S. magazine reader had seen."[18] Observed adman Jerry Della Femina: "It was the first time anyone took a realistic approach to advertising. It was the first time the advertiser ever talked to the consumer as though he was a grownup instead of a baby."[19]

The success of the Volkswagen ads brought DDB another lucrative account—Avis, the car rental company and a distant second in market share to the industry's leader, Hertz. The first ad in DDB's Avis campaign seemed to break all the rules of advertising by bragging about its second-place status: "Avis is only No. 2 in rent-a-cars. So why go with us?" The answer made advertising history and generated millions in new business for Avis: "We try harder." "Nobody had ever seen advertising like this," Juliann Sivulka wrote in her cultural history of American advertising, *Soap, Sex, and Cigarettes*. "Imagine a company admitting that it ranked only second in its industry. Further, the scrappy ads broke the taboo against comparative advertising."[20]

The Volkswagen and Avis accounts brought DDB other lucrative and high-profile clients (among them, United Airlines, Seagram's, Sony, Gillette, and Mobil Oil) and turned Bernbach, already a force in his industry, into a legend. Bernbach not only defied established creative standards but also recruited talented people rejected by other agencies because of their ethnic or religious backgrounds. Perhaps what most distinguished DDB's work was Bernbach's desire to use his ads to stimulate an emotional response. "You can say the right thing about a product and nobody will listen," he said. "You've got to say it in such a way that people will feel it in their gut. Because if they don't feel it, nothing will happen."[21] It was just this approach to advertising that attracted John Kennedy's attention.

In September 1963, Kennedy instructed his brother-in-law and newly appointed campaign director, Stephen Smith, to open discussions with DDB and other agencies about handling the advertising for his reelection campaign, as a client of the Democratic National Committee (DNC). Of the "Think small" ad, a DNC staff member later said, "It was the kind of thing that appealed to [Kennedy's] sense of humor."[22] In the fall of 1963, under Smith's direction, DNC staffers contacted several prominent advertising firms to solicit proposals for the presidential campaign account.[23] Bernbach and his partners were Democrats, and, although their firm had never handled a political campaign, they were acutely interested in the account.[24] Kennedy, of course, died before the DNC hired a firm to handle the 1964 campaign, and the task then fell to representatives of the new president.

DNC officials were making their decision to hire an advertising firm in the midst of a decade-long debate among certain politicians, social and political scientists, journalists, and advertising executives who questioned the wisdom of allowing professional advertising firms to become intimately involved in political campaigns. "Essentially, media consultants were technicians who purchased the air time, checked the lighting, supervised the make-up, arranged the set, and timed the speech," Kathleen Hall Jamieson noted in her history of presidential campaign advertising, *Packaging the Presidency*. "They played little role in the planning of the campaign. Often they did no more than produce live televised speeches." By 1960, Jamieson wrote, "a separate agency had never been spawned simply to create a campaign." That was changing rapidly and, with it, the dynamics of who controlled the campaign's message.[25]

Within the advertising profession, executives were themselves divided over the question of whether their profession could, and should, alter or craft the image of a political candidate. "There are those who say that advertising men know nothing about politics and should stick to their soap and toothpaste," *New York Times* reporter Peter Bart wrote in October 1963. "And there are those who say that ad men know so much about how to manipulate mass emotions that they endanger democratic processes." Today—when candidates spend hundreds of millions each election cycle on television, radio, and internet advertisements—it seems a quaint argument. In 1963, however, it was not unusual to fear, in Bart's words, "that ad men have attained such proficiency at the art of mass persuasion that they may put an ineffectual or evil candidate over on the American people."[26] Advertising and public relations professionals had been involved in presidential campaigns for decades, but it was television's advent and its potential to reach millions of viewers using compelling visual, as well as verbal, messages that caused renewed consternation.

While President Harry Truman had been the first presidential candidate to make a paid televised appearance (to a very small audience in 1948), the next election in 1952 gave birth to modern televised spot advertising in presidential campaigns. Dwight Eisenhower's advertising consultant, Rosser Reeves—then with the advertising firm Batten, Barton, Durstine and Osborn (BBD&O)—had persuaded his candidate to tape a series of fifteen-second television commercials—"Eisenhower Answers America"—in which he took questions from average Americans. The distasteful experience had prompted Eisenhower, between takes, to shake his head and mutter to an aide, "To think that an old soldier should come to this."[27] While Eisenhower might have found the process degrading, it proved less offensive than the prospect of losing the election, which might explain why his campaign hired three advertising agencies.[28] He submitted to the indignity of allowing Reeves to treat him and his candidacy as a product. Eisenhower's success over Illinois governor Adlai Stevenson—who mostly eschewed thirty- and sixty-second television spots for long, dry televised speeches—ushered in the advent of television as an influential force in presidential politics. Stevenson was decidedly among those who rejected this new development in politics. "This idea that you can merchandise candidates for high office like breakfast cereal—that you can gather votes like box tops—is, I think, the ultimate indignity to the democratic process," Stevenson said in his acceptance speech to the Democratic National Convention.[29]

Later, Stevenson naively predicted that Eisenhower's more professional and media-driven campaign would fail. "I don't think the American people want politics and the Presidency to become the plaything of the high-pressure men, of the ghost writers, of the public relations men," he said in Ohio. "I think they will be shocked by such contempt for the intelligence of the American people. This isn't a soap opera, this isn't Ivory Soap vs. Palmolive. This is a choice for the most important office on earth and I think the people want the candidates to talk sense about the issues."[30] Stevenson's speechwriter, George Ball, who would later serve in Lyndon Johnson's State Department, publicly decried the Reeves-produced spots. He lamented that Eisenhower's advisors "have invented a new kind of campaign—conceived not by men who want us to face the crucial issues of this crucial day, but by the high-powered hucksters of Madison Avenue."[31] Stevenson, therefore, largely rejected spot advertising in favor of preempting scheduled television broadcasts to deliver thirty-minute speeches. In 1952, after once such prime-time preemption, a telegram arrived at Stevenson's headquarters: "I like Ike and I love Lucy. Drop dead."[32]

As much as candidates like Stevenson might have disliked the idea of turning over parts of their candidacy to advertising men, the change was inexorable, if not painful and frightening. Bart, the *Times* reporter, wrote: "Now that television has become the critical medium in political warfare, politicians increasingly will have to seek the technical aid of advertising men who presumably know and understand the complex medium. To some degree, at least, candidates from now on will be 'sold' like toothpaste, and people hungry for political power will doubtless bear in mind that Madison Avenue knows a great deal about toothpaste."[33]

Journalists and statesmen were not the only ones concerned about the marriage of professional advertising and politics; some in the advertising industry worried that political advertising, as *Advertising Age* would put it in a 1973 editorial, would "blacken the other eye of the ad business."

Some advertising firms specifically rejected political work. "A political account takes three times the effort," a California advertising executive explained to *Time* in 1964, "three times the time, three times the wear and tear." As early as 1958, many advertising executives admitted to anxiety over the potential consequences of political advertising. Seventy-one percent of the 408 account executives surveyed by the advertising industry publication *Printer's Ink* agreed that "political advertising has at times overstepped the bounds of truth and taste."[34]

Among those worried about the effects of selling candidates as products was Columbia University psychologist Joost A. M. Meerloo, who decried the growing influence of "public-opinion engineers" in his 1956 book, *The Rape of the Mind: The Psychology of Thought Control, Menticide, and Brainwashing.* "The specialists in the art of persuasion and the molding of public sentiment may try to knead man's mental dough with all the tools of communication available to them: pamphlets, speeches, posters, billboards, radio programs, and T.V. shows," Meerloo warned. "They may water down the spontaneity and creativity of thoughts and ideas into sterile and streamlined clichés that direct our thoughts although we still have the illusion of being original and individual."[35]

It is likely that Meerloo, who died in 1976, would instantly recognize the early twenty-first century dysfunctional and antidemocratic political morass as the very situation he predicted, in which the political heroes are not the policy makers but the experts in spin, image manipulation, and "issues management." Despite his prescient warning, the marriage of advertising and the relatively new medium of television would prove irresistible. In 1950, only 4.2 million American homes, or 9 percent, had at least one television set. By 1960, that number had ballooned ten times to 45.2 million and, by 1964, to 51.3 million. By 1964, 92 percent of American homes had a television, a tenfold increase since 1950.[36] "Television," two political historians of the era observed, "quickly acquired a remarkable capacity for creating and changing the national mood, for making heroes and for destroying them, for showing humanity's deepest compassion and its darkest evil. The television networks were just that: networks. They linked American citizens."[37] Whether selling toothpaste or political candidates, television quickly became the medium that reshaped into its own image not only politics but also American society. Therefore, it was only natural that among the first tasks of the nascent Lyndon Johnson presidential campaign, in the months after Kennedy's death, was that of deciding who should craft Johnson's television image for the 51 million households that watched all manner of broadcasts each day.

Despite its spectacular reputation, by February 1964, DDB's prospects for landing the DNC account had waned. Some DNC staffers who had gradually accepted the involvement of an advertising firm in their campaigns were nonetheless accustomed to firms that worked for small commissions and dutifully carried out creative decisions that emanated from DNC headquarters. Working with DDB, a creative juggernaut, would be a different proposition altogether; turning over creative control to a New York advertising firm was less than appealing to some DNC staff members. Another mark against DDB was that it was known to charge more for its services than other firms—party officials were particularly worried about money in early 1964—and some of the other firms had existing relationships with DNC members. It also did not help that several of the DNC's information bureau employees were former newspapermen who had little regard for the efficacy of television advertising in politics.

Shirley Robson, who interviewed DDB executives for her 1966 master's thesis about the 1964 campaign, observed, "The politicians and the newspapermen had little understanding of advertising and the vagaries of television. These old-timers not only resented the new-fangled ad men, they feared them. They feared their political world would be tainted by the stigma of Madison Avenue and sinister ad men whose only goal is to 'sell the product.'"[38]

For their part, DDB executives were not so eager to win the account that they would compromise their standard business practices. Other advertising firms were willing to absorb production costs in order to win the account. DDB was not. In fact, as Robson learned from interviews with agency and party officials, DDB's reaction to the DNC proposal on production costs "ranged from open-mouthed amazement to frostily raised eyebrows. The agency made it quite clear that it did not do business in this way. It further made it clear that the Democratic National Committee would be just another client."[39]

Primarily because they believed DDB's advertising proposal was too ambitious for an incumbent president assured of victory, DNC treasurer Richard "Dick" Maguire and chairman John Bailey opposed hiring DDB. In 1956, the DNC had spent $1.4 million for television advertising. Four years later, the committee spent $2.4 million on behalf of Kennedy. Now, it was likely that DDB's plans included spending far more than what the DNC spent four years earlier. To Maguire and Bailey, the firm was just too expensive. "Dick felt the election was so secure," then-DNC public affairs officer Sam Smith told Robson, "that he didn't think we needed to spend the money."[40]

The official DNC ambivalence to DDB began to change in March 1964 when Johnson's aide Bill Moyers recruited his friend Lloyd Wright to serve as media coordinator for the DNC. Wright had served as public relations director for the Southern Baptist Convention and later as associate director of public affairs for the Peace Corps, the position Moyers occupied before he became the agency's deputy director. An avid student of advertising, Wright was intimately familiar with and admiring of DDB's work, especially the firm's ads for Volkswagen and Avis. Wright also believed strongly in the need to hire a respected firm to handle the campaign's media. He judged Bernbach as "one of the most creative minds I think I was ever associated with."[41] Most important, Wright was willing to pay for Bernbach's services. "You get what you pay for," Wright insisted. With Johnson and Moyers's backing, Wright would get what he wanted.[42]

Eventually, Wright winnowed the list of acceptable firms to three and, finally, two—DDB and the Chicago-based Grant Advertising. "I have counseled with the most respected men in the industry about this matter," Wright wrote in a March 11, 1964, memo to Moyers and other White House staff members, "and without exception, they say DDB is by far the best." Noting that Grant might have been somewhat less expensive because of its different fee schedule, Wright concluded: "DDB is today recognized as one of the top agencies in the business. They have a proven record of performance. Grant has been up and down for the past several years." In the end, Wright confidently concluded that DDB was not only a better, larger, and more experienced agency; the firm—with eight hundred employees—"has a staff which would be available to use for about any services we would require."[43]

Later, even Goldwater's speechwriter and advertising director, Charles Lichtenstein, would acknowledge the wisdom of Wright's selection of DDB. "Johnson's campaign made a brilliant choice," he said. "They were brilliant. I'm not so sure our agency had quite the same skills at the same level of polish . . . At that time I didn't have much experience with TV. I didn't look at it very much. I didn't even like it very much. I was an amateur in the technique of political advertising on TV."[44]

Wright later said his decision in favor of DDB was confirmed during an Oval Office meeting with President Johnson. When Johnson began to instruct Bernbach about how he might produce a certain spot, Wright observed an "anticipatory grin" spread across the adman's face. "Your job, Mr. President," Bernbach replied, "is to tell us what to say. Our job is to tell you how to say it." Johnson, Wright recalled, accepted Bernbach's admonition "quite generously."[45]

After that, Johnson seemed to give DDB wide berth to do its job. During a White House session in the summer of 1964, the firm showed him and aides several early versions of a "nuclear responsibility" film. Johnson reportedly asked a few questions, then said, "You know what you're doing" and left the meeting. DDB executives were chagrined at the brief and terse encounter, but Moyers and Valenti assured them that the meeting had gone well: "If he hadn't liked them [the films] he would have said so."[46]

The DNC and DDB signed a contact on March 19 and, by month's end, agency officials met with Moyers and other senior Johnson aides to begin mapping advertising strategy.[47] By April DDB assembled a separate forty-person, self-contained ad agency made up of art directors, copywriters, TV producers, and support staff headed by tall, affable forty-one-year-old James Graham, a recent recruit from the firm of Benton and Bowles. Graham, in fact, was not actually a full-time employee of DDB at the time Bernbach gave him the account. He was simply "borrowing" an office from the firm when he was given the opportunity to manage the president's advertising. Graham was a former military band singer, fired by his former firm in 1962 for ignoring the agency's chain of command in pitching a slogan directly to the CEO of Texaco. The CEO loved the slogan—"Trust Your Car to the Man Who Wears the Star" became the company's signature line for decades—but the Texaco marketing director who had rejected it was furious and persuaded Benton and Bowles to fire Graham.[48]

Graham's ad hoc agency was soon functioning out of office space separate from DDB's main New York headquarters, a twenty-cubicle space on the seventh floor of 20 West 43rd Street. (DDB occupied the 20th to 29th floors of the same building.) DDB also opened a satellite office in

DNC office space in downtown Washington. Among the other executives assigned to work on the DNC account were senior art director Sidney Myers, TV producer Aaron Ehrlich, and copy supervisor Stanley Lee. None had ever worked in a political campaign. "They were coming in with real fresh eyes," Graham's assistant, Ann Barton, later recalled. "They were very non-political."[49] They were, however, in Bernbach's words to a White House aide, "ardent Democrats who are deadly afraid of Goldwater and feel that the world must be handed a Johnson landslide." Taking the Johnson campaign was not entirely without potential negative consequences for DDB. "To play our small part in the achievement of such a victory," Bernbach later told a Johnson aide, "we risked the possible resentment of some of our giant Republican clients (I personally told one it was none of his business when he phoned me about our action) and we had to turn away companies who wanted to give us their accounts on a long-term basis."[50]

Graham recalled that he immersed himself in politics and public affairs to prepare for the campaign. "The very first thing I did was to start reading," Graham told *New York Times* writer Pete Hamill in October 1964. "I had never worked on an account like this before and had really never been involved in politics. Politics had interested me, of course, the way it does anyone who reads newspapers and magazines. But when I came to this, I realized how little I knew. I learned more in two months about American history, political institutions and government than I had in the previous 40 years." Graham also admitted to the initial awe he experienced when he went to see Johnson for the first time. "I know this sounds corny," Graham said, "but the first time I walked into that White House to see the President of the United States, I got a hell of a tingle." Once the tingle passed, Graham insisted that he approached the account like any other, although it is doubtful he would have considered going around Moyers to pitch ad ideas directly to Johnson, as he had done with the Texaco CEO. "The way an agency functions with a political party is not much different from the way it functions with any other account," Graham told Hamill. "They know what they want to say, and we know how to say it."[51] That is not to say that Graham and his team were completely dispassionate about their product. "Everyone was a true believer," Myers later said. "Yeah, it was like a crusade."[52]

At some point in the early days of the planning for the fall campaign, an employee posted a calendar in the hallway of the DDB seventh-floor office. Every day, someone crossed off the date with a red grease pencil. The calendar made clear the target of the campaign—Election Day, November 4. In that space, instead of the numeral 4, was a Photostat of a crowd scene. In the picture was a person holding up a sign with one word: "Peace." Johnson had not yet decided to escalate the war in Vietnam, so it is unlikely the DDB had in mind peace in Vietnam. More likely, the photo hinted at the advertising campaign Graham and his colleagues were busy crafting—one that would, in ways just as creative and innovative as the firm's iconic Volkswagen ads, revolutionize American political advertising.[53]

A series of fifteen-second spots for Dwight D. Eisenhower's 1952 campaign ushered presidential politics into the television age. In the "Eisenhower Answers America" spots, the former general appeared to take questions from average Americans. The distasteful experience prompted Eisenhower, between takes, to mutter, "To think that an old soldier should come to this." (Courtesy of the Dwight D. Eisenhower Presidential Library)

President John F. Kennedy meets with Soviet leader Nikita Khrushchev at a summit in Vienna in June 1961. Under their leadership, the United States and Russia would clash several times in the early 1960s—in Berlin and, most notably, in 1962 over Soviet nuclear missiles installed in Cuba. (Photograph from the U.S. Department of State in the John F. Kennedy Presidential Library and Museum, Boston)

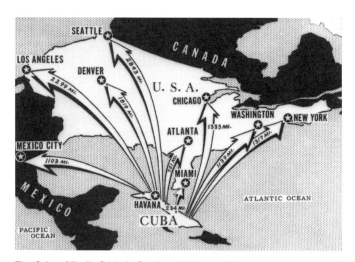

The Cuban Missile Crisis in October 1962 brought the world to the brink of nuclear war. U.S. officials regarded the long-range Soviet nuclear missiles in Cuba as a potential threat to much of the continental United States. (Courtesy of Bettmann/Corbis)

William Bernbach, the creative force of Doyle Dane Bernbach, the advertising firm that helped revolutionize advertising in the late 1950s and early 1960s, meets with Lyndon Johnson at the White House in 1966. On contract with the Democratic National Committee, DDB produced advertising for Johnson's 1964 presidential campaign. (LBJ Library photo by Yoichi Okamoto)

Think small.

18 New York University students have gotten into a sun-roof VW; a tight fit. The Volkswagen is sensibly sized for a family. Mother, father, and three growing kids suit it nicely.

In economy runs, the VW averages close to 50 miles per gallon. You won't do near that; after all, professional drivers have canny trade secrets. (Want to know some? Write VW,

Box #65, Englewood, N. J.) Use regular gas and forget about oil between changes.

The VW is 4 feet shorter than a conventional car (yet has as much leg room up front). While other cars are doomed to roam the crowded streets, you park in tiny places. VW spare parts are inexpensive. A new front fender (at an authorized VW dealer) is

$21.75.* A cylinder head, $19.95.* The nice thing is, they're seldom needed.

A new Volkswagen sedan is $1,565.* Other than a radio and side view mirror, that includes everything you'll really need.

 In 1959 about 120,000 Americans thought small and bought VWs. Think about it.

"Think Small" and "Lemon" were two early print advertisements for the German automaker Volkswagen produced by Doyle Dane Bernbach in the early 1960s. The revolutionary ads helped establish the Volkswagen Beetle as an iconic and popular automobile among American drivers and attracted the attention of President John F. Kennedy, who considered hiring the company to produce advertising for his reelection campaign. (Used with permission of Volkswagen Group of America, Inc.)

Lemon.

This Volkswagen missed the boat.

The chrome strip on the glove compartment is blemished and must be replaced. Chances are you wouldn't have noticed it; Inspector Kurt Kroner did.

There are 3,389 men at our Wolfsburg factory with only one job: to inspect Volkswagens at each stage of production. (3000 Volkswagens are produced daily; there are more inspectors than cars.)

Every shock absorber is tested (spot checking won't do!), every windshield is scanned. VWs have been rejected for surface scratches barely visible to the eye.

Final inspection is really something! VW inspectors run each car off the line onto the Funktionsprüfstand (car test stand), tote up 189 check points, gun ahead to the automatic brake stand, and say "no" to one VW out of fifty.

This preoccupation with detail means the VW lasts longer and requires less maintenance, by and large, than other cars. (It also means a used VW depreciates less than any other car.)

We pluck the lemons; you get the plums.

Avis is only No.2 in rent a cars. So why go with us?

We try damned hard. (When you're not the biggest, you have to.)

We just can't afford dirty ashtrays. Or half-empty gas tanks. Or worn wipers. Or unwashed cars. Or low tires. Or anything less than seat-adjusters that adjust. Heaters that heat. Defrosters that defrost.

Obviously, the thing we try hardest for is just to be nice. To start you out right with a new car, like a lively, super-torque Ford, and a pleasant smile. To know, say, where you get a good pastrami sandwich in Duluth.

Why?

Because we can't afford to take you for granted.

Go with us next time.

The line at our counter is shorter.

In 1962, Doyle Dane Bernbach produced its first print advertisement for Avis, the nation's number-two car rental company. The ads exhibited an honest and witty approach to advertising rarely seen until firms like DDB began stressing creativity over research. (Courtesy of Avis)

The sixty-second "Peace, Little Girl" campaign spot, also known as "Daisy Girl," was produced by Doyle Dane Bernbach for President Lyndon Johnson and shown on NBC on the evening of September 7, 1964. (Courtesy of the LBJ Library and Democratic National Committee)

The second spot in Lyndon Johnson's 1964 television campaign aired on September 12, a week after the Daisy Girl spot appeared. As another little girl devoured an ice cream cone, a female announcer asked in an urgent tone: "Do you know what people used to do? They used to explode atomic bombs in the air. Now, children should have lots of vitamin A and calcium, but they shouldn't have any Strontium 90." (Courtesy of the LBJ Library)

Another of DDB's spots took advantage of Goldwater's statement that "sometimes I think this country would be better off if we could just saw off the eastern seaboard and let it float out to the sea." The ad firm produced a Styrofoam cutout of the United States floating on water. A submerged saw slowly sliced the eastern seaboard until it went splashing into the water. (Courtesy of the LBJ Library)

Senator Barry Goldwater of Arizona, the 1964 Republican Party nominee for president. (Courtesy of Arizona Historical Foundation)

President Lyndon Johnson and Republican senator Barry Goldwater, Johnson's eventual opponent for president, meet at the White House in early 1964. (LBJ Library photo by Yoichi Okamoto)

President Lyndon Johnson and his White House press secretary, George Reedy. (LBJ Library photo by Yoichi Okamoto)

Presidential advisors Richard Goodwin (*left*) and Bill Moyers in the Oval Office with President Lyndon Johnson. Both advisors played key roles in the development of Johnson's 1964 campaign strategy. (LBJ Library photo by Yoichi Okamoto)

Jack Valenti was one of President Lyndon Johnson's most valued political advisors and a key political strategist during the 1964 presidential campaign. (LBJ Library photo by Yoichi Okamoto)

Lloyd Wright, the former Peace Corps public affairs executive, served as media coordinator for the Democratic National Committee in 1964. Wright acted as intermediary between the White House and the campaign's New York advertising firm, Doyle Dane Bernbach. (Courtesy of Lloyd Wright)

Tony Schwartz and his daughter Kayla. Schwartz's creative and groundbreaking work with sound recordings in the 1950s and 1960s helped provide the inspiration for the Daisy Girl spot. Schwartz, on contract with Doyle Dane Bernbach, provided much of the spot's soundtrack. (Courtesy of Anton Schwartz)

Sidney Myers was senior art director at Doyle Dane Bernbach in 1964 and a key member of the firm's special team that produced the Daisy Girl and other television spots for Lyndon Johnson's 1964 presidential campaign. (Courtesy of Sidney Myers)

Senator Barry Goldwater on the campaign trail in 1964 with his wife Peggy. (Courtesy of Arizona Historical Foundation)

Lyndon Johnson addresses a campaign rally in Rhode Island on September 28, 1964.
(LBJ Library photo by Cecil Stoughton)

Republican presidential nominee Barry Goldwater concedes the election to President Lyndon Johnson on November 4, 1964. (Courtesy of Arizona Historical Foundation)

4 THESE ARE THE STAKES

Lyndon Johnson was worried about his reelection—that is, worried about the prospect that he might not earn a historic landslide victory. A Gallup poll released on July 10, 1964, that showed him with the support of 77 percent of voters, to Barry Goldwater's 18 percent, did little to assuage his anxiety.[1] "I hate to tell you this," a sullen Johnson told his press secretary, George Reedy, on July 20, "but it's my considered judgment, in the light of what I see happening and what I have heard, and people I have talked to in whom I have confidence, that we wouldn't carry a state in the South if the vote were tomorrow." Reedy agreed—and they were both largely correct. (Johnson would lose the Deep South: Louisiana, Mississippi, Alabama, Georgia, and South Carolina.)[2] Aide Bill Moyers recalled that Johnson "could be a 'nervous Nellie' on this; he had been dubbed 'Landslide Lyndon,' you'll recall, and he never took a campaign for granted." Recalling Johnson's eighty-seven-vote victory to the U.S. Senate in 1948, Moyers continued, "So although there was no serious reason to think he would lose, he wanted a real—not an 87-vote—landslide this time. He wanted a mandate to complete the New Deal and a Congress to deliver it."[3]

Gallup's new numbers would not be released until late July, but they would certainly give Johnson even more reason for concern. Numbers gathered by the polling firm during July 7–10 showed the race "narrowing." Goldwater, who now polled at 26 percent, had cut Johnson's numbers down from their stratospheric high of 77 to a more plausible 62 percent.[4] Johnson wasn't the only one nervous about the election. Some supporters, observing the fervor of Goldwater's supporters in California and other places, began to wonder if they were witnessing the high-water mark of the Arizonan's candidacy or the beginning of a tidal wave. "I suggest it is time someone said to the President what apparently no one has yet said to him—that he could lose this election," Johnson aide Henry H. Wilson wrote to his White House colleague Lawrence O'Brien on July 8.

"I suggest that we're facing a situation brand new in American politics and that we're going to have to throw all the old rules out of the window and play it by ear." Wilson was not urging Johnson to attack Goldwater but strongly argued that "other Democrats should be scientifically dissecting him. And if there is a movement afoot to stockpile and pass out this ammunition systematically I haven't come across it."[5]

Several weeks later, a similar warning arrived at the White House. "I'm afraid Democrats don't realize that unless President Johnson fights a tough, no-holds-barred campaign, he's going to lose the election," California advertising executive Norman Maher wrote Johnson aide Jack Valenti on July 20, the same day that Johnson confessed to Reedy his worries about losing the South. In his nine-page letter, Maher—who was apparently not an intimate of Valenti or any other Johnson administration official—volunteered his ideas for a strong attack on Goldwater's extremist positions and rhetoric. Among his proposals was an idea to exploit Goldwater's troubling rhetoric on nuclear weapons. "Show a nuclear bomb blast," Maher advised. "Then ask, 'Do you want anyone other than the President of the U.S. to have control over our nuclear weapons?'" Among the slogans Maher suggested was, "Prevent Nuclear Holocaust. Let's think from the head—not shoot from the hip. Vote Democratic."[6] It is not clear what, if any, reply Maher's letter prompted, but he was likely channeling the fretfulness of Johnson and some of his aides.

Other advisors were more sanguine. "It begins to look as though the Republicans are really going on a Kamikaze mission in November," Brandeis University political scientist John P. Roche told Moyers in a June 12 letter. "This puts the President in a wonderful strategic position: he can play the campaign with lofty statesmanship[,] ignoring the fact that Goldwater exists." Yet, even Roche—who was also president of Americans for Democratic Action and who would later join Johnson's White House staff—advised using the campaign to keep the pressure on Goldwater. "At the next level, we can really run a savage assault: A billboard, e.g., can be devised reading 'Goldwater in 64—Hotwater in 65?' with a mushroom cloud in the background." Moyers shared the memo with Johnson.[7]

Talk of going at Goldwater by suggesting he was an unstable man who, if elected, would start a nuclear war was not confined to unsolicited counsel in letters from outside advisors. That notion was not so far-fetched to anyone who read comments Goldwater's wife Peggy and others made to writer Alvin Toffler of *Good Housekeeping* that were published in May 1964. One theme of the article was Goldwater's volcanic temper. Peggy acknowledged, "He still flies off every once in a while." A lifelong friend, Harry Rosenzweig, was quoted saying that Goldwater "has a tendency to get irritated and blow his top." Toffler quoted a close friend of Peggy's, Eleanor Libby, who said, "He scares everyone in the family except Peggy." But the most damaging comments came from Peggy herself, who described what Toffler characterized as Goldwater's "nervous breakdown" in 1937 and another one two years later. "His nerves broke completely," Peggy said, explaining that a long rest helped Goldwater recover from the first bout and a trip to Hawaii helped him overcome the second.[8]

In his July 20 phone conversation with Johnson, Reedy broached the issue of Goldwater's temperament. "Now, I think there's a weakness to Goldwater," Reedy said. "I think the big weakness is people think he's pretty reckless. And I think the one thing we oughta get at now is some of the things he's said about the nuclear test ban treaty, but not say it in the way they've been said. I think we've gotta get this down to some gut things." Johnson continued listening, without comment, as Reedy continued.

Mothers that are worried about having radioactive poison in their kids' milk. Men that are worried about becoming sterile. Uh, give 'em some thoughts about maybe kids being born with two heads and things like that. And that, my God, you're going to have this reckless man who shoots from the hip and who talks first and thinks afterward. You're going to give him sole authority to decide these things. I know it's a little bit tough . . . But, you know, that's something that unites everybody. Doesn't matter whether they're North, South, East or West. No mother wants her kid drinking milk with poison in it. No man wants to think, my God, he [Goldwater] gets all excited, and Khrushchev gets all excited, and we start testing [nuclear weapons]. You may have to talk about war. That's a mistake they've made so far. They start all this testing stuff, I might walk around and just be denutted. And then you start talking about kids with two heads, and stuff like that.

Johnson abruptly cut Reedy off and changed the subject. Before they ended their conversation, however, Johnson insisted, "We're not going to do anything to incite or inflame anybody." Reedy may have concluded that Johnson did not agree with his advice, but the president had clearly heard Reedy's counsel. In a phone conversation the following day with Attorney General Robert Kennedy, Johnson discussed their concern that Goldwater might make the election a referendum on Johnson's support for civil rights legislation. "If it comes down to the question of civil rights," Kennedy observed, "the Democrats are going to have a very tough time."

Johnson agreed but turned the conversation to how to prevent Goldwater's attacks on civil rights from gaining traction. "What we need to get in on is [Goldwater's] impetuousness and his impulsiveness and his wanting to turn the Bomb over to somebody else," Johnson said (a reference to the controversy over Goldwater's statements about giving control of tactical nuclear weapons to the NATO commander). Kennedy agreed. "I think that will scare people and I think that is helpful." Kennedy, however, argued that the issue was, perhaps, too complex for the average voter and that basic economic issues—"what is this going to mean as far as your lunch pail is concerned"—might have more resonance. "When the country is at peace, as it is now, they're not concerned about Russians as much. There's not a crisis like the Berlin Wall or Cuba." Johnson pushed back. "I don't know," he replied, then echoed Reedy's advice of the previous day. "A mother is pretty worried if she thinks her child is drinking contaminated milk or that maybe she's going to have a baby with two heads. [Goldwater's] pretty vulnerable."[9] That observation, seemingly an echo of Reedy, comported with Johnson's general view of the race. "Men worry about heart attacks," he once told a group of aides, clutching his chest. "Women worry about cancer of the tit. But everybody worries about war and peace. Everything else is chicken shit."[10]

At a Cabinet meeting the following day, Johnson brought along his anxiety about Goldwater's threat, noting a significant increase of his strength in the South and observing, according to one participant, that "Goldwater had more things going for him than we realized." Agriculture Secretary Orville Freeman noted that Johnson was "quite concerned, quite apprehensive, and quite tense" about Goldwater's potential in the fall elections. For now, at least, Johnson told his advisors, he did not favor a full-frontal attack on Goldwater, preferring to take the high road.[11]

Some of Johnson's high-road talk may have been a masquerade or an indication that he was not yet fully comfortable with the thought of attacking his opponent and that he worried whether it would appear undignified or telegraph a sense of panic. It is more likely that he had no compunction about attacking Goldwater; he simply did not want to do so directly, unless absolutely necessary. What is very clear is that Johnson wanted a landslide victory that would give him a mandate—making Kennedy's victory, in Johnson's words, "look like a pathetic peep."[12] Explaining the White House campaign advertising strategy that Johnson approved and that DDB began implementing, Richard Goodwin observed, "Translated into more conventional political terms it meant that we would open the campaign with an assault designed to put Goldwater on the defensive, and then, as he struggled to extricate himself, withdraw to the high ground of constructive statesmanship."[13]

For months, with the White House's blessing (but with little consultation or direction from Johnson or his aides), DDB executives had been preparing an aggressive fall television campaign. Incredible as it may sound, DDB executives insisted that they never viewed any of the spots that Kennedy had used four years earlier. "We felt that campaign was different from almost any other in recent years," James Graham told the *New York Times* in October 1964. "For one thing, L.B.J. took over from a martyred President. Therefore, the ideas and style of the two men had to be indicated. For another, it has been many years since the lines of American political arguments have been drawn so sharply. And yet, there are hazards involved. The lines can shift suddenly and sharply." For example, Graham explained, the agency had initially planned to make civil rights a major theme of the fall advertising. "The Civil Rights Bill had not been passed, and to some of us it seemed as if Johnson had an awful lot of lose by pushing it through," Graham said. "I was frankly awed by his courage. We had prepared a lot of material on civil rights then, expecting it to be a big issue." When the bill passed Congress in July, the issue disappeared as a viable campaign issue, despite Goldwater's negative vote.[14]

In late March, the agency had presented its preliminary media proposal to DNC officials, which included "our additional goal to create a landslide, a mandate, which will also produce a Democratic House and Senate." Besides civil rights, the agency proposed two broad themes for the advertising campaign: peace or war and future well-being. As the Republicans had not yet nominated their candidate, DDB initially focused on developing broad, general strategy, not specific messages. Executives proposed advertising primarily on television, both national and local, in "12 critical states," supplemented by radio and newspaper advertisements. The total estimated cost for network spots was $1.39 million, with an additional $696,000 recommended for local TV spots. DDB recommend another $1.6 million in newspaper advertisements. At least one person at the White House regarded the proposed TV budget as far too small. "*Not enough* double—triple—quadruple," one aide, perhaps Moyers, scribbled on the memo.[15]

By late July, after some acrimonious debate between DDB and DNC officials, the outlines of the fall campaign, and its specific messages, took shape. Those at the DNC who favored a more modest advertising campaign found themselves overruled and marginalized by White House officials—particularly Moyers—who, with Wright's assistance, had seized control of the party's media operation.[16]

Instead of running local spots in twelve states, Johnson's aides expanded the battlefield to twenty-eight. The overall television budget grew from the modest $1.6 million that DNC had originally proposed to an astonishing $6.25 million.[17] Attacking Goldwater for his reckless rhetoric about nuclear weapons was not among the subjects DDB had first proposed to the DNC in mid-June. Instead, a June 11 DDB memo indicates the firm was beginning work on storyboards for spots on poverty, education, medical care, foreign affairs, civil rights, the history of the Democratic Party, and the Johnson administration's accomplishments.[18] (DDB's work also included designing the arena for the Democratic National Convention to be held in Atlantic City. To DNC officials' horror, the agency proposed dispensing with the traditional bunting and balloons. DDB, instead, designed large billboards to remind the national television audience about various aspects of Johnson's Great Society. DNC officials insisted on modifying the design to include two huge photographs of Johnson.)[19] A month later, however, after a meeting with White House officials, including Bill Moyers, Jack Valenti, and Richard Goodwin, the plan for spots expanded and now included at least two spots relating to "peace," an indication that the White House was planning to broaden the campaign, not just geographically but also on the issues.[20] "We had instructed [DDB] that Goldwater's casual approach to the use of nuclear weapons," Goodwin recalled, "together with the militance of his Cold War rhetoric, was to be a major theme of our television campaign since it undermined public confidence in that 'wise restraint' which was the most important quality expected of a president in the atomic age." Johnson, as usual, put it more descriptively: "It's a very big bus and we're all in it. People want to be sure that the man at the wheel isn't going to drive it over a cliff."[21]

Johnson and his aides also began approving specific concepts for spots and began setting the course for what Johnson's campaign would say about Johnson and Goldwater in its early television advertising. "We worked day and night," Sidney Myers recalled. "We were traveling back and forth to Washington on the train, staying at the White House, having brainstorming sessions with Lloyd Wright and Bill Moyers."[22]

Despite all this activity, Johnson and his advisors had not yet given clear instructions to DDB about when it could begin producing all the TV spots it was developing, except to inform the agency in mid-August that it planned to scale back its television campaign by eliminating spots in local markets (a somewhat perplexing decision, given that Johnson owned a television station in Austin, Texas). Johnson may have been heeding counsel from his close friend and advisor John Connally, the governor of Texas, who strongly urged Johnson to limit his campaign activity to official pronouncements from the White House. For a brief time, at least, Johnson seemed to accept the advice. From the Oval Office one day that summer, Johnson looked out to the Rose Garden and told several aides, "That's where I'm going to run my campaign this fall."[23]

Johnson's temporary inclination to campaign above the fray prompted DDB's Bernbach to write a worried letter on August 17 to Moyers: "If a decision isn't taken immediately to activate the television advertising plans, there might be serious consequences to the campaign," Bernbach wrote. "This is no time for me to be tactful with you. There is too much at stake." Worried that Johnson might wait too late to begin advertising on television, Bernbach admonished:

> We agreed that a very necessary part of the campaign is that part devoted to exposing to the voting public the absurd, contradictory and dangerous nature of the opposition candidate. It was agreed that this part of the campaign should be undertaken immediately following our Convention. It is already apparent that Barry Goldwater is making every effort to adjust his extreme position to one more acceptable. Knowing the short memory of the average person, it is entirely possible he might succeed in creating a new character for himself if we are unable to remind people of the truth about this man.[24]

Asked in 2009 about Johnson's diffidence about the television advertising campaign, Moyers recalled, "LBJ wasn't sure he even needed to spend much money on advertising to beat [Goldwater], and he himself was uncertain that TV ads, still in their infancy . . . would make any difference."[25]

What appeared to shake Johnson from his lethargy was concern over renewed Republican momentum following a highly publicized meeting on August 6 between Goldwater, former president Dwight Eisenhower, and former vice president Richard Nixon at Eisenhower's Gettysburg, Pennsylvania, farm. The following week, in nearby Hershey, Goldwater had attended a meeting with a larger group of Republican leaders, at which Eisenhower, who had earlier expressed doubts about the Republican nominee, strongly affirmed his support for Goldwater. Not long thereafter, three southern Democratic governors endorsed Goldwater, and a fourth said he would not do so only because he did not believe he could win.[26]

Johnson's unwillingness to launch his television advertising, and his instructions to aides about taking the high road, did not deter him from attacking Goldwater on August 15. After Goldwater, in Hershey, suggested (falsely) that Johnson had authorized the use of nuclear weapons against North Vietnam following the early-August attack on a U.S. naval vessel by a North Vietnamese boat in the Gulf of Tonkin, Johnson hit back hard and sought to reinforce Goldwater's reputation for recklessness. "Loose charges on nuclear weapons without any shadow of justification," Johnson said from the White House Rose Garden, "are a disservice to our national security, a disservice to peace and, as for that matter, a great disservice to the entire free world."[27]

Goldwater's aggressiveness and the emerging Republican harmony seemed to spur Johnson's campaign into motion. On August 31, Moyers finally received Johnson's permission to pull the trigger on the television campaign. Once he decided to proceed, Johnson went all out. Johnson approved $2 million in TV spots, with an additional $2.5 million in local television advertising and $500,000 for radio. That was the beginning of what Johnson planned to spend on television advertising. "In addition," Moyers reported to the DNC's treasurer, Richard Maguire, "the President said he would be willing to add another 15 fund raising dinners if you believe these are necessary—five for him and ten for Humphrey."[28]

Although Johnson had temporarily put the spending on hold, the planning for the television campaign had never stopped. DDB was ready for battle. One of the firm's first products, produced in July, was a four-minute spot, "Confessions of a Republican," in which a man, approximately thirty-three years old, would face the camera and confess his concerns about Goldwater. "He is against the whole idea of peaceful coexistence," the man would say, adding later, "I wish he was against *war* as strongly as he's against some of these other things. I wish he had the imagination to just close his eyes, just *picture* what this country would look like after a nuclear war."[29] A week later, in early August, DDB executives were back with storyboards for a raft of spots. Among those rejected by Moyers and others was a spot titled "Kremlin Men's Room" (an obvious reference to Goldwater's offhand remark about lobbing a nuclear warhead into the Kremlin).[30]

The first spot envisioned, however, was only sixty seconds long and was named, simply, "Peace, Little Girl." The original DDB script for this spot does not appear to be among the papers of the DNC on file at the Lyndon B. Johnson Library; but in its ultimate form it was very simple. DDB envisioned an innocent little girl in a sun-splashed field, with the sound of birds chirping in the background. In her hands, the little girl held a daisy. In her own voice, she would be counting as she plucked the petals, "One . . . two . . . three . . . four . . . five . . . seven . . . six . . . six . . . eight . . . nine . . . nine." At the end of her count, the girl would look up, somewhat startled, as if she had heard a distant sound. The camera would freeze on the girl's face and move into an extreme close-up of her eye, as another voice abruptly entered the spot. As if being broadcast from a loudspeaker at a missile test site, this man would begin counting down in an urgent tone: "Ten . . . nine . . . eight . . . seven . . . six . . . five . . . four . . . three . . . two . . . one." At that point, the camera would quickly zero in on the girl's dark eye, which would fill the screen, now replaced with the sound and visual fury of a sudden atomic bomb explosion. As the fiery mushroom cloud consumed the screen, Johnson's voice would enter the spot: "These are the stakes—to make a world in which all of God's children can live, or to go into the dark. We must either love each other, or we must die." The spot would end with these words flashed on the screen, "Vote for President Johnson on November 3," as the announcer said, "Vote for President Johnson on November third. The stakes are too high for you to stay home."[31]

It is not entirely clear how the spot, later known as "Daisy Girl," was born. It is clear, however, that the idea of using an atomic bomb blast in a spot was something that had occurred to several people who offered their advice to the White House. While it is not likely the idea for the Daisy Girl spot originated in the White House, it is apparent that Johnson and his aides, during the late spring and summer of 1964, grew increasingly open to the idea of a devastating attack on Goldwater for his statements and positions regarding nuclear war.

Creating a spot to graphically and effectively communicate Johnson's view of Goldwater's recklessness was on the minds of DDB copywriters and art directors in the summer when they contacted a well-regarded, reclusive New York sound man to consult with them on about a half-dozen television spots.

Tony Schwartz was a forty-year-old Manhattan-born artist and ad man whose long-held fascination with sound had earned him a reputation as a wizard of sound and sound effects. Early in his career, an heir to the Sears-Roebuck fortune began supporting Schwartz's groundbreaking sound work, freeing him to ramble around New York with a sixteen-pound, battery-operated, Webster Webcor wire recorder, capturing the many sounds of his vibrant neighborhood. "Advertisers, to this day," Schwartz wrote in 1973, "look perplexed when I tell them I have no interest in *sound effects*. I am solely interested in the *effect of sound* on people [emphasis Schwartz]."[32] Over time, Schwartz released nineteen long-playing record albums featuring the sounds he had recorded. Adding to his renown, beginning in 1945, he hosted a popular New York radio program, "Around New York," on WNYC, on which he featured his recordings. (The show lasted until 1976.) Schwartz also engaged in early versions of performance art by presenting his recordings to audiences at art museums and nightclubs. Eventually, he returned to advertising.

Famously agoraphobic, Schwartz rarely left his Hell's Kitchen home alone. Those who desired his services came to him. Hundreds of corporate and political clients made the trek to see Schwartz, not just because of his groundbreaking work with sound but because of his belief in using emotions rather than rational appeals to persuade. One example of his approach was embodied in a famous 1963 public service announcement (PSA) he produced for the American Cancer Society. Over video of two children dressed in their parents' clothing, the announcer said, "Children love to imitate their parents. Children learn by imitating their parents. Do you smoke cigarettes?" Schwartz was also the first advertising man to use real children's voices in his ads, a distinction that undoubtedly attracted the attention of DDB executives as they conceived the "Peace, Little Girl" spot.[33]

Sometime in the summer of 1964, DDB executives contacted Schwartz. "They had an approach for a five-minute spot on the nuclear war issue," Schwartz later recalled, "with voices counting down in English and Russian; they wanted to know what to do for a sixty-second version." Schwartz, who was fascinated with the sound of numbers, had produced radio and TV spots that featured countdowns. In 1960, he had used the voice of his nephew counting out of order for a Polaroid commercial. In 1962, Schwartz produced a nuclear disarmament PSA for the United Nations (UN) in which a child (his nephew) counted out a series of numbers, followed by an adult who counted down, NASA-style, before the sound of an atomic blast. At the end, an announcer declared, "Young and old. Another world war means death to us all. Support the United Nations." The first part of the UN PSA, which aired on WNYC radio, is remarkable in its similarity to what would eventually be called the "Daisy Girl" spot. In addition to those two spots, Schwartz had also used a countdown track in a demo reel for IBM that featured the sound of various numbers.[34]

When the DDB team of Sidney Myers, Aaron Ehrlich, Stanley Lee, and Gene Case visited Schwartz's home, he played them the raw tape of his nephew counting. "We heard it and it was so striking and then we said, 'Wow, wouldn't that be great,'" Myers later recalled, adding that he believed Lee, then said, "Wouldn't it be great to have this countdown and then meld it into an ominous voice of a guy counting down and the bombs exploding." Schwartz, of course, had produced just such a spot— his UN PSA.[35]

What happened next is a point of contention between Schwartz and DDB that continued until Schwartz's death in June 2008. Schwartz always maintained that he conceived the spot and was the driving force behind its production. Schwartz told one historian that he had not only conceived the spot but also given specific directions to DDB on how to film it: "You have a little child pulling the petals off a daisy. The camera goes into the center of the daisy, and that becomes the explosion when it detonates."[36] (Actually, the camera zoomed into the center of the girl's eye, not the daisy.) In a letter to the *New York Times* in 2000, Schwartz described himself as "the creator of the original 'Daisy' advertisement in 1964" and, in defending the spot, referred to "my own ad."[37]

DDB's Myers recalled matters quite differently. He maintained that it was his idea to slowly zoom into the girl's eye, insisting that he copied the technique from French filmmaker François Truffaut's iconic 1959 movie, *The 400 Blows*. As Myers recalled:

> At the end of that movie, the little boy is running and stops and freezes and I think that the camera moves into his face—I don't think it goes into his eye. And I saw that movie and it struck me so . . . it was such a powerful image that I thought it would be a great image to do on this commercial. The idea of freezing her and moving into the eye didn't happen until we saw the film that we shot of just the girl standing in the field. And it was a wide shot. We thought that it would be very powerful just to move into her face and then move into her eye and then just dissolve to an explosion. And I *know that was my idea.*[38]

When cultural historian Bill Geerhart asked who developed the basic concept for the spot, Myers responded, "I really don't know. It could have happened back at the agency between Stan and I. I know that Stan and I were responsible for producing and creating the commercial. Nobody else was around when that happened. So, it was either Stan's idea or my idea." Interviewed in 2010, Myers gave Schwartz a bit more credit for the spot. "He certainly had a lot to do with it because he did the soundtrack and that's where we got the concept from, the idea," Myers said. "But he did not do any of the residual work; he did not come up with the idea to use it as a commercial for Johnson." Myers insisted it was Schwartz's counting soundtrack that sparked the idea for the spot but that it was not Schwartz's idea—nor did he participate in producing the spot beyond providing sound. "We did the rest of it," Myers said. "We shot it. We edited it. We came up with the idea of zooming into her eye and exploding the bomb. That was all Doyle Dane Bernbach, not him." Myers also insisted that Schwartz was not present when he and other DDB executives filmed the spot in August of 1964. "He was nowhere near the shoot."[39]

Myers did acknowledge that the idea for the Daisy Girl spot came after the visit to Schwartz's home. That, coupled with the striking similarity of the UN spot to the Daisy Girl spot, lends credence to Schwartz's contention that he was instrumental in the spot's conception. "The evidence seems unquestionable that Schwartz was responsible for providing the audio roadmap for the spot," Bill Geerhart concluded after his investigation. At the very least, Schwartz appears to deserve a bit more credit for the spot than Myers and other DDB executives were willing to give him.

One additional bit of circumstantial evidence in Schwartz's favor is that DDB executives did not begin publicly challenging Schwartz's recollection of his role in producing the spot until the early 1990s—and then did so with a vengeance.[40]

In DDB's favor is a lengthy article about the firm's role in the campaign's advertising, published in the *New York Times Magazine* in October 1964. The piece, by Pete Hamill, never mentions Schwartz. Just as intriguing is that Schwartz apparently did not contact the *New York Times* to assert his role, nor did he publicly challenge the story. In fact, it was not until 1968, in a *Washington Post* story, that Schwartz became identified as the creator of the Daisy Girl spot.[41] In addition, Schwartz's name was not among those DDB employees listed when the firm and the spot won the Art Directors Club's annual "Distinctive Merit Award" in 1965 (nor did he protest his exclusion as an award recipient).[42]

Nonetheless, Schwartz's contributions to the concept of the spot, especially its soundtrack, seem clear. "The visual component, however, is another story," Geerhart concluded. "The conceptualist for the brilliant scenario of the innocent child in the field of daisies is either Tony Schwartz or it is the DDB team (Sid Myers & Stanley Lee). With both sides claiming credit and neither possessing any conclusive evidence, this is a dispute unlikely to ever be resolved."[43]

However it was created, and whoever was responsible, the White House approved the spot, along with several others, in early August and DDB scheduled it for filming shortly thereafter. Sometime that month, in New York's Highbridge Park, near the banks of the Harlem River on Manhattan's northernmost point, DDB assembled a crew to film a freckled-faced, three-year-old, brown-eyed redhead from Pine Beach, New Jersey, who wore a simple summer blouse adorned with a print of small teddy bears. Monique Corzilius (she used the stage name Monique Cozy) was a budding child actor who had appeared in a Lipton Soup print ad the month before and would later star in ads for Kodak, SpaghettiOs, and Kool Pops. The youngest of the three daughters of Fred and Colette Corzilius, Monique was not the child her mother thought most likely to become a child actor when she brought the little girl and her sisters into New York for auditions in early 1964. However, the girl's distinctive red hair and brown eyes made her a standout among the many blonde and brunette children who showed up for casting calls. DDB executives selected Corzilius after auditioning as many as thirty other child actors.

On the day of the shoot—no one remembers the exact date—she sat patiently before the whirring camera and plucked petals from a dandelion (not a daisy, as legend has it) and counted from one to nine (it was not, technically, a countdown). After a long day of shooting, requiring at least twenty takes, during which the director initially prompted her to "count for me, sweetheart," filming wrapped. Days later, in the New York offices of Elliot, Unger and Elliot, a commercial production firm, editors joined footage of Monique's counting with the image of an exploding nuclear bomb. To that, they added the sound provided by Schwartz— the mission-control counting and Johnson's admonition "we must either love each other or we must die." That line was from a 1939 poem by W. H. Auden, "September 1, 1939," in which one of the final lines is, "We must love one another or die."* DDB had taken Johnson's voice quoting Auden's line and the rest of his portion of the spot's narration—"These are the stakes, to make a world in which all of God's children can live, or go into the dark"—from an April 17, 1964, speech delivered in the White House Rose Garden. Exactly who chose this sentence for inclusion in the spot was the subject of dispute among Schwartz and DDB executives. In 1994, Schwartz told *Audio* magazine that he selected the passage from five hours of Johnson speeches delivered to him by the White House. Myers, however, claimed that Stanley Lee discovered the passage, while yet another DDB executive, Gene Case, also claimed the decision.[44]

Sometime in August, Lloyd Wright traveled to DDB's New York office to see a collection of spots. Among them was the Daisy Girl spot. "Here was an image of innocence and vulnerability, of peace, something to warm the heart of the viewer," cultural historian Paul Rutherford wrote later. "It might evoke actual memories, or ersatz memories, the kind put in place by movies, television programs, and other ads." Interrupting that idyllic scene was the atomic blast, "leaving the impression," Rutherford wrote, "that the little girl and her world had been obliterated."[45] DDB's Jim Graham said he believed the Daisy Girl was so effective because of the way it reduced the "general" to the "specific." As he later explained, "Genocide—such as Hitler's murder of millions—is too immense a concept for people to grasp. But *The Diary of Anne Frank* tells it all."[46]

"Wow," Wright recalled thinking at the time. "That is powerful."

*Outraged by Johnson's use of the line, which Auden himself had disowned by the mid-1940s, Auden wrote to a friend: "One cannot let one's name be associated with shits" (Richard Davenport-Hines, *Auden* [New York: Pantheon, 1999], 319).

Asked in 2010 if he immediately perceived the impact the spot would have, Wright said, "Yes. It was just so powerful, I felt that it was going to achieve its goal."[47] On August 20, DDB executives brought the finished spot to the White House for a showing attended by, among others, Johnson, Moyers, Goodwin, Valenti, Wright, Bernbach, and James Graham. "We watched with mounting jubilation," Goodwin recalled. "After the viewing room lights went up, the advertising executive [probably Bernbach] looked with anxious uncertainty toward his momentarily silent and expressionless audience. Finally, a voice was heard—I think it was Bill Moyers's—'It's wonderful. But it's going to get us in a lot of trouble.' He was expressing what we all knew."[48] Whatever angst the group was feeling quickly disappeared. The DDB memo produced after the meeting indicated that "the President expressed some dissatisfaction with the quality of his voice reproduction."[49] White House officials, however, approved the spot without edits. "They were very good clients," Sidney Myers recalled, adding that other clients would often suggest changes. "They never got involved in that. They just okayed the concept and this [Daisy Girl] was it." Graham echoed Myers's view of the White House as a hands-off client. "The one thing I learned from working with serious politicians," he said in 1964, "is that you have to know the terrain yourself. You can't wing it. It has to be your own baby, all the way down the line, or the consistency and the general impact suffers."

Myers recalled that Johnson, after viewing the Daisy Girl spot, simply said, "Good job, boys."[50]

Four days later, DDB set in motion the process of buying airtime for the spot, at a cost of $24,000,** during NBC's "Monday Night at the Movies" on the night of September 7—a night that, quite literally, would transform American political advertising.[51]

**A subsequent report by *Newsweek*, however, put the cost of airing the spot at $30,000 ("Spotting the Candidate," *Newsweek*, Sept. 21, 1964).

5 THE HOMES OF AMERICA ARE HORRIFIED

Johnson and his advisors instinctively knew that the Daisy Girl spot would create a sensation and that much of the reaction to it would be adverse. More cautious than Johnson's younger, more-aggressive aides, advisors like Clark Clifford and some DNC officials worried about the Daisy Girl spot and other hard-hitting, edgy DDB spots. Johnson's men, however, would take the calculated risk that they could safely push the edges of political advertising and the limits of good taste.[1]

"We all realized it would create quite a reaction," Lloyd Wright recalled, adding in a subsequent interview that the campaign's strategy was to first define Goldwater "as too impulsive to trust with the nation's defense systems, using his own words to illustrate the point." The second stage, Wright explained, "was to posit LBJ as the experienced, thoughtful, analytical opposite, imminently trustworthy on defense issues and committed to achieving what would later be known as a 'Great Society' domestic agenda." Wright confessed that, instead of fearing a backlash against the negative advertising, they feared that the first two stages of their strategy would succeed so well that "voter apathy might limit turnout."[2]

In another interview, Wright admitted that a potential backlash did worry some Johnson aides, "but we judged it to be so effective in pursuit of our strategy that any risk involved was worth taking."[3] Johnson aide Richard Goodwin later recalled, "The spot was a winner, but it would almost certainly be attacked as 'unfair,' even 'dirty politics,' by establishment pundits and publications." Goodwin and the others concluded that "a few objections were meaningless, but a sustained attack on our campaign tactics would ultimately be taken up by the rest of the media—including television commentators, whose views were invariably derived, after some time for reading and discussion from the 'bellwether sheep' of their profession."

To avert a media backlash, Johnson's men developed the following strategy: "We would saturate prime-time viewing hours for a few days (or more, if we could get away with it)," Goodwin recalled, "and then respond to the inevitable protests by withdrawing the spot." Goodwin imagined the conversation he or another staff member might have with a reporter: "It seems fine to us, but if that's how you feel about it, Mr. Reston [or Mr. Sulzberger . . . or Mr. Bradlee], we won't use it anymore."[4]

Also in the spot's favor was the clever way that DDB had conceived it. As psychologist Drew Westin observed in his 2007 book, *The Political Brain: The Role of Emotion in Deciding the Fate of the Nation*, DDB insulated the Johnson campaign from the worst possible criticism by the way it carefully positioned the president in the spot. While Johnson's voice and name were present, like all the nineteen other twenty- and sixty-second spots DDB produced for the campaign in 1964, the spot did not show the president's image. (While absent from DDB's spots, Johnson would appear in several four-minute and half-hour programs during the campaign's final weeks.)[5] That eliminated the *visual* association of him with the incendiary subject of nuclear war. Westin also noted that Johnson's language "invoked God and love, even though they ended with a frightening warning. It is difficult to see this as a 'hateful' message." While certainly a negative spot, Westin believed that "central to its power is a message designed to resonate with people's love of their children, families, and God." Finally, as many others have noted, Westin observed that the spot never mentioned Goldwater.[6]

DDB scheduled the spot to air the day that Johnson would formally inaugurate his fall campaign—Labor Day, Monday, September 7. That day, in Detroit before a crowd of 100,000 in Cadillac Square, Johnson tore into Goldwater's views about the acceptability of using "conventional" nuclear weapons, thereby setting the stage for the very unconventional campaign weapons he would deploy on national television that evening. In his speech Johnson insisted, "Make no mistake, there's no such thing as a 'conventional nuclear weapon.'" Reminding the crowd that the U.S. had not used nuclear weapons in nineteen years, Johnson said, "To do so now is a political decision of the highest order. It would lead us down an uncertain path of blows and counterblows whose outcome none may know." Referring to Goldwater's disputed remarks about giving the NATO commander the authority over use of certain nuclear weapons, Johnson said, "No President of the United States can divest himself of the responsibility for such a decision." The speech, despite its grave subject matter, did not resonate with the crowd. A *New York Times* reporter noted, "As he spoke, mostly in abstractions, his listeners were stirred only to occasional desultory applause. They were not moved."[7] That evening's paid, televised message from Johnson, as Johnson's people knew, would certainly not be abstract. And it would, they were confident, resonate with millions of Americans.

NBC's main prime-time fare that evening was its popular "Monday Night at the Movies," which the network had inaugurated the year before and would soon move to Wednesday nights. The program would run until 1999 and featured edited versions of major motion pictures and, later, made-for-television movies. On the night of September 7, 1964, NBC broadcast the 1951 film *David and Bathsheba*, starring Gregory Peck and Susan Hayward. Sometime around 9:50 P.M. Eastern time, the Daisy Girl spot aired. By one estimate, as many as 50 million viewers saw the spot. Among those who did not see it were the parents of the little girl who plucked the flower petals. At their home in Pine Beach, New Jersey, Fred and Colette Corzilius had no idea that the spot their daughter had taped earlier in the summer was for Lyndon Johnson. They had no inkling that the girl's counting would be linked with a nuclear explosion. Until shocked family and friends began to call their house that evening, they had no idea that their daughter's image—and her imaginary nuclear annihilation—had been witnessed by 50 million television viewers. It seemed they had never thought to ask DDB executives about the nature of the commercial—a rookie mistake they would not make again.[8]

At the White House, the response was immediate. According to Moyers, the White House switchboard lit up with calls of protest. Johnson, too, began getting calls from friends concerned that the spot had gone too far. The critics included several guests who were at the White House for a small, late-evening dinner. Johnson interrupted the meal to phone Moyers, who was still in his West Wing office. Despite the ostensible urgency of the call, Moyers sensed immediately that Johnson "was having a wonderful time putting on an act" for the benefit of his dinner guests. "What the hell do you mean putting on that ad that just ran?" Johnson asked. "I've been swamped with calls, and the Goldwater people are calling it a low blow." Moyers recalled that Johnson's "voice was chuckling all the time."*

*In this instance, Moyers's recollection may have been faulty. It is not clear how Johnson would have already heard reaction from Goldwater's campaign, which apparently did

Summoned to the White House's second-floor living quarters for further discussion, Moyers recalled that he arrived around 10 P.M. to find Johnson and his friends still at dinner. "Don't you think that was pretty tough?" Johnson asked, for the benefit of his guests. "Mr. President," Moyers replied, "we were just reminding people that at this time it might be a good idea to have an experienced hand on the button." Moyers said he assured Johnson that the ad would not run again. As he began to leave, Moyers said that Johnson followed him toward the elevator. "You sure we ought to run it just once?" Johnson asked. Moyers said that he assured him once was enough.[9]

Years later, Moyers was not sure if the decision to air the spot only once was made before September 7. "At the time, early in the campaign, I don't think we planned anything beyond one shots, as we were feeling our way every day," he recalled in 2009. "The response to it made up our minds: there was no need to repeat it."[10] Others, including Lloyd Wright, recalled tentative plans to run the spot several more times. The fact that all three television networks subsequently aired the ad during their nightly news broadcasts made the decision to cancel it much easier. *Time* featured an image of the Daisy Girl on the September 25 cover of a special "Nuclear Issue." Of the TV news reports about the spot, Wright said, "My impression was that we would have liked to run it again and because of the reaction, I suggested to Bill [Moyers] that maybe we don't need to run it again." Wright added, "We weren't unhappy to pull it because it had done its job, we thought."[11]

Contributing to the media attention the spot received was the Goldwater campaign's decision to react strongly to a spot that did not mention its candidate by name nor show his image—a strategy that ultimately attracted more media attention to the spot and invited analysis about its meaning. On September 12, Republican National Committee (RNC) chairman Dean Burch—who said the RNC fielded 1,300 protest phone calls—filed a formal complaint with the Fair Campaign Practices Committee, a private nonpartisan organization, supported by leaders of both political parties, which devoted itself to persuading candidates to subscribe

---

not issue a statement about the spot on the evening of September 7. On another occasion, Moyers recalled that during his initial phone call with Johnson, the president observed, "But I guess it did what we Goddamned set out to do, didn't it?" (Kathleen Hall Jamieson, *Packaging the Presidency: A History and Criticism of Presidential Campaign Advertising* [New York: Oxford, 1996], 200).

to its Code of Fair Campaign Practices. "This horror-type commercial is designed to arouse basic emotions and has no place in this campaign," Burch wrote to committee chairman Charles P. Taft. Burch demanded that the committee "call upon the President to halt this smear attack on a United States Senator and the candidate for the Republican Party for the Presidency." Burch wrote that the Daisy Girl spot "is only one in a series intended to smear the Republican candidate. The campaign represents a new low in American Politics and violates the American sense of fair play and good taste." Burch closed his letter with his own emotional appeal: "I know of one case where a child watching this Johnson spot was so violently upset that she cried and had nausea all night. I am asking the networks to take this spot off the air as a matter of common decency."[12]

The same day, Everett Dirksen, the Republican Senate leader, complained about the spot to the National Association of Broadcasters (NAB). "In light of this commercial, I would hope that you would read again the [NAB] Code of Ethics and ask yourself whether you agree that this is unfit for children to see and takes the level of political campaigning to a depth never before approached in the history of television." Several days later, a NAB official responded that "we have never considered the application of [the NAB Television Code] to political announcements [which] involves issues not present in other forms of television advertising."[13] In a speech on the House floor, Republican leader Charles Halleck of Indiana demanded that Johnson cancel the spot and complained, "Decent people resent this kind of play on emotions, this appeal to fear, this scare campaign that outdoes a horror movie." In the Senate, Republican Thruston Morton of Kentucky attacked "President Johnson's effort over national television through paid time to win the election by scaring the wits out of children in order to pressure their parents." Morton entered the text of the spot into the *Congressional Record* and demanded that Johnson "end these despicable acts of cowardice," adding, "Are you proud, Mr. President?"[14]

Johnson's team saved the networks the trouble of debating continued broadcasts of the spot. The campaign had no need to air the spot again. The RNC was now helping them publicize it. "Everything they did to keep the story going, we applauded," Lloyd Wright recalled. "We observed it with glee." Wright believed the wiser response from the Goldwater camp would have been "to shut up about it. Ignore it."[15]

"What is amusing now but wasn't then," Goldwater's media strate-gist Charles Lichtenstein acknowledged, "is that we gave the daisy ad so much publicity that it was shown over and over again on news and com-mentary programs so a lot of people saw it who wouldn't have ordinar-ily seen it. We thought it was very damaging so obviously we demanded that it be withdrawn."[16]

At the White House, Johnson's aides were more than happy to pretend that they had magnanimously agreed to withdraw the spot. Even John-son's running mate, Hubert Humphrey, played along, telling the moder-ators of NBC's "Meet the Press" on September 20, "I did not approve of the TV spot," and adding, "I did not personally think it was very good." That disclaimer out of the way, Humphrey took advantage of the oppor-tunity to remind viewers that Goldwater "did once say that he thought it would be well to use nuclear weapons to defoliate . . . the jungles of Viet-nam."[17]

Goldwater waited until late September to weigh in. "The homes of America are horrified and the intelligence of Americans is insulted by weird television advertising by which this administration threatens the end of the world unless all-wise Lyndon is given the nation for his very own," he said at a rally in Indianapolis.[18] For all his fury at the time over what he regarded as an unethical cheap shot, Goldwater later paid trib-ute to the spot, even while damning it. "LBJ had very little difficulty, with the aid of the Democratic National Committee and his campaign public relations people, in creating a caricature of Goldwater which was so gro-tesque that, had I personally believed all the allegations, I would have voted against my own candidacy," Goldwater wrote in 1970. "In this, the Democrats' course of action was simplicity itself." While protesting that the Johnson campaign's argument against him was a collection of "com-pletely false and ridiculous charges," Goldwater was surely correct when he observed, "the campaign against me was based on one element—fear."[19] (In a 1988 memoir, Goldwater's assessment of the spot was much harsher: "Those bomb commercials were the start of dirty political ads on television. It was the beginning of what I call 'electronic dirt.'")[20]

Fair or not, the Daisy Girl spot had accomplished exactly what DDB, Johnson, and his staff had intended. The spot, Moyers told Johnson in a September 13 memorandum "caused [Goldwater's] people to start de-fending him right away. Yesterday Burch said: 'This ad implies that Sen-ator Goldwater is a reckless man and Lyndon Johnson is a careful man.'

Well, that's exactly what we wanted to imply. *And we also hoped someone around Goldwater would say it, not us.* They did. Yesterday was spent in trying to show that Goldwater *isn't* reckless."[21]

Moyers was correct. The Goldwater camp had taken the bait and would continue to call attention to the spot. The day of Moyers's memo, the director of radio-television for the RNC, Edward Nellor, told the *Chicago Tribune* that the Daisy Girl spot could endanger more than Goldwater's candidacy. "An unbalanced person who sees the ad could very well say, 'No one is going to do that to little girls or my girl,' and make an attempt on Goldwater's life."[22] As late as October 5, the assistant RNC chair, Pat Hutar, described the spot for an audience and asserted that it "states that the election of Sen. Goldwater will be the same as a declaration of war. It clearly implies he is a warmonger."[23] After the campaign, DDB's James Graham acknowledged the helpfulness of Goldwater's allies who repeatedly came to their candidate's defense but helped Johnson by committing one of the cardinal sins of political communication—repeating your opponent's allegation. "We are humbly grateful," Graham later said, "to the Senator's Republican colleagues for giving us the two big campaign issues—the bomb and Social Security . . . There is no weapon so effective as the words of one's 'friends.'"[24] Journalist and campaign historian Theodore H. White agreed, noting that "the shriek of Republican indignation fastened the bomb message on [Goldwater's campaign] more tightly than any calculation could have expected."[25]

Beyond the fulminations of Burch, Dirksen, and other GOP leaders, the ad seemed to catch Goldwater and his aides unaware, despite a detailed (if not entirely accurate) description of the spot published the week before in a front-page story in *Advertising Age:* "It opens with an appealing three-year-old child walking blissfully through a field. She picks the petals from a flower, counting them as they fall. The picture switches to the countdown for a missile. In the background, President Johnson talks about the danger to our children unless nuclear power is controlled." The story even informed readers exactly when the spot would run—"in the 9:50–9:55 period (EDT) on NBC's 'Monday Night at the Movies.'"[26]

The spot also found its way to the front page of the *Wall Street Journal* on August 28, in a story that forecast, in great detail, the Johnson campaign's advertising strategy. "In contrast to the coolly complimentary role being readied for the President, the image-makers engaged by the Democrats are out to depict Barry Goldwater as a belligerent hothead," reporter Jerry Landauer wrote from Atlantic City as the Democratic National Convention ended. "They seek, moreover, to insinuate into public consciousness that the Republican nominee is tied in with 'extremists' and segregationists." Among the "samples" of DDB spots that Landauer cited: "On television, an American voice breaks the somber silence overhanging an atomic test site with a slow countdown: the count ends in a mushroom cloud."[27]

While these were not exact descriptions of the Daisy Girl spot, it is difficult to believe that Goldwater's advisors could not have anticipated some form of attack centered around the question of Goldwater's intemperate remarks about nuclear weapons. Their actions in mid-to-late September, however, indicate that they were not entirely certain how to respond. Theodore White observed that Goldwater "seemed so stunned, so shocked by the attack on him as a killer, that he could not clear his mind to guide a counterattack."[28] Tony Schwartz later ventured that instead of trying to prevent the Johnson campaign and the networks from showing the spot again, "Probably the smartest thing Goldwater could have done at the time was to agree with the attitude of the commercial and offer to help pay for running it. This would have undercut the sensational effect of it and possible won him many votes."[29] As difficult as it is to imagine Goldwater adopting that strategy, Schwartz's intuition may have been correct. The spot's real punch was its shock value, combined with frantic GOP protestations that gave voice to the unstated message of the spot. As Schwartz recognized, had the Johnson campaign aired the spot continually for several weeks, the repetition would have resulted in the audience's habituation, that is, a psychological process in which a stimulus (the shocking juxtaposition of the little girl and the nuclear explosion) loses its power to astonish or terrify. "Living in constant fear is exhausting and makes normal functioning impossible," science writer Rush W. Dozier observed in his book *Fear Itself.* "If we cannot habituate, then psychological problems—diseases of fear—may cripple our lives."[30] Put another way, in the case of the Daisy Girl spot, familiarity might not have bred contempt but, rather, ambivalence. Habituation, however, may be avoided if the stimulation (fear of Goldwater blowing up the world) is varied. Therefore, instead of showing the Daisy Girl spot a dozen times, DDB devoted its subsequent spots to evoking fear of Goldwater for a handful of other reasons. (Graham, however, could not resist taunting the Goldwater camp with the prospect that the Johnson campaign might revive the Daisy Girl spot for one last showing prior to the election. In the October 25 *New York Times Magazine* story about DDB's role in the campaign, Graham reiterated that the campaign believed that the spot "had outlived its usefulness," but added, "we might run our little girl again before Nov. 3."[31]

Johnson and his advisors were not about to entrust the work of destroying Goldwater entirely to the Republican nominee's allies. In the wake of the Daisy Girl spot and the media attention it earned, the Johnson campaign worked to press its advantage. "We ought to treat Goldwater not as an equal, who has credentials to be President," Valenti told Johnson in a September 7 memorandum, "but as a *radical,* a preposterous candidate who would ruin this country and our future." To do this, Valenti advised "maintaining in the public mind the firm fear that Goldwater as President would be a vast national joke if it weren't so dangerous to imagine. If we treat him seriously, we will surely lose support." To further undermine Goldwater's credibility, Valenti suggested "humor, barbs, jokes, ridicule."[32] A week later, Valenti urged Moyers and others not to allow Goldwater's radical image to "get all smoothed up to our detriment. Right now, the biggest asset we have is Goldwater's alleged instability [regarding the] atom and hydrogen bombs. We MUST NOT let this slip away." Into every Johnson speech, Valenti urged putting the term, "A-Bomb Barry," and, he added, the Johnson campaign should "deny him any right to be called sane or stable."[33] That day, Lloyd Wright chimed in, in a memo to Moyers, with thoughts on additional themes for television spots, among them, "He [Goldwater] could have his finger—or that of some field commander—on the nuclear trigger. That's what he wants to do."[34]

In that spirit, Johnson's next television salvo, aired on "NBC Saturday Night at the Movies" on September 12, featured another little girl, this one exploiting fears of the adverse health impacts on children if a President Goldwater restarted nuclear testing. In this spot—"Little Girl, Ice Cream Cone"—the girl is again outside but, instead of a flower, she eagerly licks an ice cream cone while a female announcer—it was the first time a woman had provided the voice-over for a presidential campaign spot—asks in an urgent tone:

> Do you know what people used to do? They used to explode atomic bombs in the air. Now children should have lots of vitamin A and calcium, but they shouldn't have any Strontium 90 or Cesium 137. These

things come from atomic bombs, and they are radioactive. They can make you die. Do you know what people finally did? They got together and signed a nuclear test ban treaty. And then the radioactive poison started to go away.

But now there's a man who wants to be president of the United States, and he doesn't like this treaty. He fought against it. He even voted against it. He wants to go on testing more bombs. His name is Barry Goldwater, and if he is elected they might start testing all over again.[35]

DDB produced a third spot—"Pregnant Lady"—without the campaign's permission, that implied that nuclear testing might harm the unborn (perhaps a result of Reedy's and Johnson's discussion about two-headed babies). Narrated by a female announcer, a young mother and her young child stroll happily through a park to the sound of cheerful music. The announcer discusses the nuclear test ban treaty and makes the assertion that "radioactive fallout from atomic testing is a biological risk . . . President Johnson will not break this treaty."[36] "I remember telling [DDB] no, we would never do it," Wright later said, expressing his and Moyers's concern that they could not prove a connection between testing and birth defects. "Bombs do blow up people, so the daisy ad was based in reality but this ad was going beyond the realm of accepted reality," Wright said. "It was straining for scare tactics."[37]

DDB's tactics clearly were designed to scare voters—and its decision to use children as the vehicle for that fear was cunningly effective. In her historical study of the use of children in political advertising, communication scholar Susan A. Sherr notes that while nuclear war would clearly kill children *and* adults, the Daisy Girl spot primarily emphasized the impact on children. "This child was clearly being used to trigger emotions different from those an endangered adult might evoke," Sherr writes. "The ad reframes nuclear defense policy as an issue of protecting children rather than a complex set of issues involving the preservation of all humanity." Furthermore, Sherr notes, using children allowed Johnson and DDB to say visually what they could not communicate verbally—"if Goldwater gets elected little girls counting flowers in fields will be blown up by nuclear bombs."[38]

Pressing its case, the Johnson campaign next aired a DDB-produced four-minute spot, "Atomic Bomb—Test Ban," that recreated a series of alternating, accelerating blasts of U.S. and Russian nuclear bombs with Russian and English countdowns. The blasts finally stop with the voice of John F. Kennedy announcing the conclusion of negotiations for the nuclear test ban treaty. The spot concludes with Johnson's voice declaring that "those who oppose agreement to lessen the dangers of war curse the only light that can lead us out of the darkness. As long as I am your president I will work to bring peace to this world and the world of our children."[39]

In another spot— "Telephone Hot Line"—that has been copied several times since 1965 (most recently in the 2008 presidential election), a phone with a flashing light, labeled "White House," rings incessantly. The phone, clearly meant to represent the U.S.–Soviet "Hotline," is not answered. The announcer concludes: "This particular phone only rings in a serious crisis. Leave it in the hands of a man who has proven himself responsible."[40]

In the campaign's final volley on the nuclear issue, a twenty-second spot, a male announcer intones over the image and sound of a nuclear explosion: "On October 24th, 1963, Barry Goldwater said of the nuclear bomb, 'Merely another weapon.' Merely another weapon? Vote for President Johnson." This spot, like all the others produced by DDB for Johnson, ended with the ominous and fear-inducing tagline: "The stakes are too high for you to stay home."[41]

Soon, some of Johnson's advisors began to fret that the stinging attacks on Goldwater, while initially effective, might backfire. "I'm worried about the count-down ad," Moyers's assistant Hayes Redmon told his boss on September 18. "We cannot let people forget [Goldwater's] nuclear irresponsibility but I'm wary about throwing more bombs around. We already have people worried about Barry the Bomber. Scare ads could have . . . an 'overkill' effect."[42] Another of Moyers's advisors, John Bartlow Martin, warned that whipping up fear over Goldwater's reckless nuclear policies was no substitute for a positive statement about Johnson's priorities in a full term of office. "[Johnson] has given the people something to vote against—Goldwater," Martin wrote in a memorandum on October 1. "Perhaps now he should give them something to vote for." Martin advised temporarily dropping the nuclear issue so that Johnson could revive it in the campaign's final week. "It is cemented in; nothing Goldwater can do will shake it. If the President keeps hitting it, it may backfire, because it's complicated. Or people may just learn to live with it, develop an immunity."[43] Several days later, advisor Lawrence O'Brien reported to Johnson that "90 per cent of the campaign leaders we talked with were critical of the television spot showing the little girl pulling petals off a daisy." O'Brien quickly added, however, that "this ad did more to crystallize public opinion against Goldwater than any other single tool we're using."[44] Three weeks later, DNC executive director Kenneth O'Donnell (who had been among Kennedy's closest advisors) told Johnson bluntly, "It is our opinion, and it is shared by all our people in the field, that our television has been most ineffective. We have used the same spots over and over until they have outlived their usefulness." O'Donnell went so far as to advise Johnson to pull down all the DDB spots and refocus the campaign's advertising on purely positive aspects of Johnson's record and legislative objectives.[45]

DNC officials favored a conservative approach, opposed to what one called DDB's "artsy" spots attacking Goldwater. In response, DDB executives and the DNC's Lloyd Wright began dealing directly with White House officials like Moyers, showing DNC staff spots they knew would not be objectionable. One DNC official later said that he saw several of the Johnson spots "so many times, I was sick of them."[46] Johnson, his aides, and Wright bypassed DNC leaders on advertising strategy for at least two reasons. First, Johnson did not trust many of the top leaders at the DNC, most of them Kennedy associates Johnson had left in place after his predecessor's assassination and who he suspected were plotting to award the 1964 presidential nomination to Robert Kennedy. "He didn't trust Dick Maguire," recalled Johnson's friend and advisor Arthur Krim, explaining that Johnson suspected the Kennedy intimates at the DNC "were just living out the days but not really loyal to [Johnson]." Second, Johnson essentially operated as his own campaign manager. It is inconceivable that someone so compulsive about controlling his political affairs would cede control of advertising to a political party dominated by people he regarded as Kennedy loyalists.[47]

Nonetheless, the criticism of the Daisy Girl spot was having some effect on Johnson, briefly shaking his confidence in DDB's aggressive advertising strategy. "I really want to play it safe," Johnson told Labor Secretary Willard Wirtz, who was intimately involved in crafting campaign strategy, on October 5. Discussing a speech on the nuclear test ban treaty with Wirtz, Johnson cautioned, "Let's be sure we don't get into something like we did on that [Daisy Girl] spot thing, [resulting in criticism] that we're overdoing it."[48]

More persuasive, to Johnson and Moyers at least, was the advice to continue driving home the fear of a Goldwater presidency. *"The campaign itself has got to keep pressing to put Goldwater on the defensive—*on nuclear bombs, his contradictions, and personality," advisor Fred Dutton wrote from DNC headquarters in late September. "Political attack is still the best defense!"[49] "Peace is a cardinal issue, especially in the Mid-West," Charles S. Murphy, the undersecretary of agriculture, wrote on September 28 when asked to produce a memorandum on the content of farm speeches. "You will probably get more votes from farm people there because they think Goldwater is trigger happy than you will on farm issues." A week earlier, after he took a trip outside Washington, Moyers had informed Johnson, Goldwater "is on the defensive on the nuclear issue (which is THE issue, I think)."[50]

So, the Johnson campaign sustained its assault. Beyond addressing nuclear irresponsibility, DDB produced spots that drove home other aspects of Goldwater's perceived recklessness and extremism. One took advantage of Goldwater's statement that "sometimes I think this country would be better off if we could just saw off the eastern seaboard and let it float out to the sea." In response, DDB produced a Styrofoam cutout of the United States floating on water. A submerged saw slowly sliced the eastern seaboard until it went splashing into the water. At the spot's conclusion, the announcer asks: "Can a man who makes statements like this be expected to serve all the people, justly and fairly?" In another spot, which featured Goldwater's remarks about changing the Social Security system, a pair of hands—presumably Goldwater's—tore in half a Social Security card as an announcer says, "Even his running mate, William Miller, admits that Barry Goldwater's voluntary plan would wreck your Social Security."[51]

The relentless series of attacks on Goldwater, however, were not confined to DDB's television ads. Although he never appeared (except for his voice) in any of the twenty- or sixty-second spots that directly or indirectly attacked Goldwater, on the stump Johnson pressed his point about his opponent's recklessness with surgical precision. While addressing a wide range of domestic issues and social concerns in most of his speeches that fall, Johnson often inserted veiled references to Goldwater that could only have reinforced the messages of his paid televisions spots.

In a speech at a Democratic Party dinner in Harrisburg, Pennsylvania, on September 10, Johnson warned about the spread of "reckless factions, contemptuous toward the will of majorities; callous toward the plight of minorities; arrogant toward allies; belligerent toward adversaries; careless toward peace." Johnson did not mention Goldwater and his supporters by name, but it was clear who he had in mind. "They demand that you choose a doctrine that is alien to America—that would lead to a tragic convulsion in our foreign relations; a doctrine that flaunts the unity of our society and searches for scapegoats among our people. It is a doctrine that invites extremism to take over our land. It is a doctrine that plays loosely with human destiny, and this generation of Americans will have no part of it."[52] In Texarkana on September 25, Johnson again assailed Goldwater: "Who leads America must speak what is deep in the hearts of Americans, not what comes from the top of the head. And deep in the heart of all America is a love for peace. We so devoutly want peace in the world. We want peace in the lives of all of our people."[53] At Johns Hopkins University on October 1: "We have in our power at this moment the ability to destroy 300 times as many human lives as were lost in the entire many years of World War II. So the purpose of our politics must be to make man's extinction improbable, and man's fulfillment inevitable."[54]

In Alexandria, Virginia, on October 6, he said: "Never before within the memory of any person here have the American people been asked to make a basic and radical departure from the beliefs and values which are the source of our economic health and our hopes for peace."[55] In Des Moines, Iowa, on October 7: "Peace, a five-letter word—p-e-a-c-e— peace is our first priority. America is the most powerful Nation in all the world, but we must use our power and our responsibility carefully and with restraint—not injudiciously, never recklessly."[56] That evening, in a nationally televised address to the nation, Johnson said: "We are told we should consider using atomic weapons in Viet-Nam, even in Eastern Europe should there be an uprising. We are told we should break off relations with Russia—and with it any hope of lasting agreement. We are urged to withdraw from the United Nations and stop our help to other countries. We have heard the test ban treaty denounced. This is the treaty that has halted the radioactive poisoning of the air we breathe. We are urged to threaten others with force if they don't do as we say. We are told, in effect, to withdraw into an armed camp—with a few carefully selected friends—and try to intimidate our adversaries into submission."[57]

In Los Angeles, on October 11, he declared: "You are not going to get peace in the world by rattling your rockets. You can't have government by ultimatum." Later that day in Las Vegas, he continued: "The issues are clear: Are we going to work together to resolve the problems that we face at home? Are we going to close our eyes and just hope they go away? Are we going to keep on seeking ways of easing world tensions and thereby reducing the dangers of nuclear war? Or are we going to repudiate those policies and walk an unknown, an uncertain and dangerous path down through the edge of darkness?" The next day, in Reno: "We here in the West know how the West was won. It wasn't won by the man on the horse who thought he could settle every argument with a quick draw and a shot from the hip. We here in the West aren't about to turn in our sterling-silver American heritage for a plastic credit card that reads 'Shoot now, pay later.'" At a rally in New York's Madison Square Garden on October 15: "Peace at home will be of little value if an impulsive thumb moves up toward the button that can destroy 300 million people in a matter of moments. Peace at home and prosperity among our people will get us nowhere if we have a government by ultimatum, and we bluff about our bombs, and we rattle our rockets around until we get into a destructive war." In Orlando, Florida, on October 26: "When you select your next President, the man who must sit there with his thumb close to that button, the man who must reach over and answer that telephone, that 'hot line,' when Moscow is calling, you want to select the person that, in your conscience, you know has the experience, has the judgment, and that you know will do what is best for his country."[58]

Finally, in an election-eve radio and television speech from the White House on November 2, Johnson said:

> We are told that tactical nuclear weapons are simply a new kind of conventional explosive. If these views prevail, if we abandon the proven principles of both parties, I have no doubt that our hopes for peace and the cause of freedom will be in serious peril. Let there be no mistake. There is no check or protection against error or foolhardiness by the President of the United States. He, alone, makes basic

decisions which can lead us toward peace or toward mounting danger. In his hands is the power which can lay waste in hours a civilization that it took a thousand years to build. In your hands is the decision to choose the man that you will entrust with this responsibility for your survival.[59]

The irony of much of Johnson's talk about peace is that he most certainly knew—or at least deeply feared—that deteriorating events in Vietnam might soon force him to escalate the U.S.-led war. Despite Johnson's soothing campaign rhetoric about wanting "no wider war," his advisors were actively planning for the very likely postelection possibility that the U.S. military would wade more deeply into Southeast Asia. Johnson's rhetoric about peace was powerful and effective, even with the somewhat-skeptical chairman of the Senate Foreign Relations Committee, J. William Fulbright of Arkansas. Johnson's personal assurances to Fulbright—"he was seeking a way to minimize the war and not to expand it and to find a solution and negotiate a settlement"—were persuasive. "I was taken in by the misrepresentations," Fulbright later said, "until it was too late."[60]

Not content with only television spots and speeches, Johnson and his aides looked for other ways to paint a picture of Goldwater as a dangerous radical and extremist and a reckless cowboy with a twitchy finger on the nuclear button. While he took the (relatively) high road in his speeches—and his aides actually quashed several DDB spots that they regarded as inappropriate, ineffective, or both—Johnson eagerly worked to solidify the image of Goldwater's extremism by encouraging associates to disseminate false rumors about his opponent. On October 10, he urged New York Liberal Party leader Alex Rose to spread word that Goldwater belonged to the far-right John Birch Society. After Rose had planted that rumor, Johnson planned to start linking Goldwater to the Ku Klux Klan. "The thing that gets you votes," Johnson told Rose, "is when they [voters] get scared about a man that's going to be a Klansmen." Johnson hoped the press would start asking Goldwater or his aides, "Is he resigning [from the Birch Society]? Will he quit it? Will he denounce it? Is it true that he's on it? Did he intend it to be against Eisenhower? What kind of a secret thing? Has he ever had any connections to the Klan?" The same day, Johnson told Moyers and another aide that his campaign should consider spreading the rumor that Goldwater was "psychotic."[61]

Along with Johnson, no one on Johnson's staff seemed to enjoy the

evisceration of Goldwater more than Moyers, who not only oversaw the
DDB account for the White House but also helped orchestrate much of
Johnson's campaign rhetoric. An ordained Baptist minister from Texas,
Moyers worked, with considerable success, to stir up religious groups
against Johnson's opponent.[62] It was Goldwater's perceived reckless attitude toward nuclear weapons, however, that ignited Moyers's considerable imagination and resulted in a series of memoranda to Johnson and
others about possible television ads and creative ways to attack Goldwater. As noted by journalist Rick Perlstein in his history of the Johnson-
Goldwater race, "Moyers was instrumental in pioneering an innovation
in presidential campaigning: the full-time espionage, sabotage, and mud-
slinging unit."[63] Known in the White House as "The Five O'Clock Club"
or "The Department of Dirty Tricks," it consisted of more than a dozen
junior staffers from various agencies who often gathered in the offices of
Johnson's special counsel, Myer Feldman, to, in Theodore White's words,
"discuss deviltry." Its purpose was counteroffensive or counterinsurgency.
"Goldwater's advance schedules were always obtained by the club," White
wrote, "so, too, somehow, were the texts of Goldwater's speeches hours
before anyone else had seen them." That meant that even before Goldwater had spoken the words at a rally, "the material to refute or contradict
him was generally in the hands of the local Democratic mayor, governor, or Congressman." Instead of waiting to rebut Goldwater in the next
day's newspaper, the Johnson campaign's response often ran in the same
edition as the report of Goldwater's speech.[64] (In its emphasis on intelligence gathering and rapid response, the Johnson operation was a pre-
cursor of the "war room" that presidential candidate Bill Clinton would
establish during his 1992 campaign for the White House.)

Among the most interesting of Moyers's machinations was his apparent success in persuading the producers of "Fail Safe" to release their motion picture prior to the presidential election. The movie, released on October 7 and based on a 1963 novel of the same name, told the story of a
breakdown in the U.S. nuclear "fail safe" protocol that prevented an accidental nuclear strike on the Soviet Union. In the movie—starring Henry
Fonda and Walter Matthau—a U.S. aircraft delivers a nuclear warhead
to Moscow, defying all attempts by U.S. and Soviet forces to stop or destroy the plane. As a result of Moscow's destruction, New York City is
also targeted for nuclear annihilation.

On September 29, Moyers told Johnson that he had obtained a copy of the film, "which we have arranged to be released in about ten days. It should have a pretty good impact on the campaign in our favor, since it deals with irresponsibility in the handling of nuclear weapons." In the end, "Fail Safe" likely had only a minor impact. The movie fared poorly at the box office, and the story itself did not feature an irresponsible president bent on nuclear conflict. Instead, the president, portrayed by Fonda, was an earnest, responsible leader. Moscow's destruction was the result of a technical glitch, not a saber-rattling president. That said, the movie, along with the release of the more popular "Dr. Strangelove"—a similarly themed movie released in late January 1964—likely added something to the public's anxiety about the risk of nuclear annihilation.[65]

Other than Johnson, no one in the White House attracted more criticism for the tone of the campaign than Moyers. "Moyers portrayed himself as a poor preacher boy," Goldwater wrote in 1988, "but he was actually involved in the dirtiest work of the Johnson campaign." Over the years, Goldwater said, he had watched Moyers, in his subsequent role as a journalist and commentator, on the CBS Evening News and on the Public Broadcasting System. "He portrays himself as an honorable, decent American," Goldwater scoffed. "Every time I see him, I get sick to my stomach and want to throw up." In his memoir, Goldwater said that Johnson's then-press secretary, George Reedy, later confided to him that "this espionage operation was silliness because we had the race won. However, some around the White House reveled in dirty tricks."[66]

In Moyers's defense, Reedy's critical comments should be viewed in light of Moyers's replacement of Reedy as White House press secretary in 1965. Furthermore, considering the illegal dirty tricks performed by the Nixon White House in the early 1970s (including the burglary of the Democratic National Committee offices), the Johnson campaign operation may be more accurately compared to the war-room/opposition research operations considered ethical, standard fare in modern political campaigns.

One area where Johnson and Moyers may have crossed the ethical line, however, was Moyers's October 26 request of the FBI, at Johnson's behest, to investigate more than a dozen members of Goldwater's staff. Documents released by the FBI to a congressional investigating committee do not indicate what Johnson and Moyers were looking for, but transcripts of White House telephone conversations suggest it related to the arrest of Johnson's closest aide. Washington, D.C., police had arrested

Walter Jenkins on October 7 on charges of engaging in homosexual sex in a YMCA men's room.[67]

In a March 1974 article in *Newsweek,* Moyers addressed the episode and suggested that Johnson was merely pursuing a suggestion by FBI director J. Edgar Hoover that Republican Party staff members working on behalf of Goldwater had entrapped Jenkins. (When asked in 2010 about the FBI request, Moyers declined comment and referred this author to the *Newsweek* article.) No evidence, however, exists that Hoover made such a suggestion to Johnson. In fact, it appears that, contrary to Moyers's assertion, Johnson himself raised the issue of an RNC-sponsored setup and was told by a senior FBI official that no evidence for such a scenario existed. Whatever useful information Moyers and Johnson had hoped the FBI might discover about Goldwater—perhaps homosexuality on Goldwater's staff—did not turn up. FBI officials reported to the White House that they found nothing incriminating.[68]

In retrospect, in a 2009 interview, Moyers expressed misgivings about the general thrust of the campaign, especially its role in casting Johnson as a peacemaker:

> In time, I came to have many reservations about the use of television, and about our own—at the time rather uncalculated—contribution to advancing the political art. Ads, of course, enable candidates to choose their message on their terms and to reach a lot of people. But they more often than not trivialize the discourse, reduce issues to black and white, and can be very misleading—deliberately or unwittingly. It disturbs me in retrospect that while Lyndon Johnson was portrayed as the peacemaker in that campaign and Barry Goldwater the war monger (based on his own remarks), it was LBJ who, after election, committed the country to a long, bloody war in Vietnam that we eventually lost. And we never touched on Vietnam in any of those spots.[69]

Since 1964, the question of ethics has been repeatedly raised by journalists, historians, and former Johnson advisors: Was it ethical to use a presidential campaign to strike fear into the hearts of American voters? Was it within the bounds of decency to suggest to parents that electing Goldwater might result in the poisoning or death of their children? Was it right to imply that Goldwater's election might bring about the destruction of the world in a nuclear holocaust? Was it beyond the bounds of decency to lend credence to suggestions that Goldwater was mentally unstable?

Lloyd Wright confessed that he later questioned whether Daisy Girl and other spots went too far. "Over the succeeding years I realized that we had overreached, probably, in painting [Goldwater] with the trigger finger concept regarding the nuclear weapon," said Wright, who acknowledged that he admired Goldwater's subsequent leadership in the Senate. "I believe the power of the commercial distorted a realistic image of who Goldwater really was. As we said, he was too quick with the lip. But I think we made him appear more dangerous than he would have been."[70]

Bruce Felknor, then the executive director of the Fair Campaign Practices Committee, wrote in his 1966 book, *Dirty Politics*, "As a matter of fact, Goldwater had created the image the Democrats were exploiting . . . But exploitation need not engender distortion. The bomb spots oversimplified grossly."[71] Oversimplification, however, is the soul of political advertising, something that would become painfully apparent in subsequent elections as the tactics employed by DDB became the norm. The Daisy Girl spot and DDB's other work stood out so prominently, and made such an impression on so many viewers, not because their messages were fundamentally unfair or false but because they were fresh. Just as DDB had revolutionized product advertising in the late 1950s and early 1960s, so its work had the same impact on political advertising. Nothing like its spots had ever been seen in American politics.

Even DDB's president and founder, Bill Bernbach, felt it necessary to defend his firm's work in a *New York Times Magazine* story on October 25, 1964: "The little girl commercial was deplored on absolutely erroneous grounds," Bernbach told journalist Pete Hamill. "The central theme of this campaign—whether you like it or not—is nuclear responsibility. Perhaps that theme is not a tasteful one; there is no way to make death pleasant. But I am satisfied that our presentation of the issue was done dramatically, truthfully, and with taste. We built an agency on taste."[72]

Johnson aide Richard Goodwin acknowledged that DDB's nuclear spots might have been "a little extravagant perhaps, but [were] within the bounds of legitimate political debate." As Goodwin explained in a 1989 book: "In dozens of statements, Goldwater had expressed his willingness to use military force in the protection of 'American interests,' had indicated that nuclear weapons were not unique but merely another weapon in the arsenal, referred to the Soviet Union as an implacable enemy bent on the destruction of freedom. If one took him seriously—and it is always a mistake not to take a man's statement of convictions seriously—then he was a very dangerous man." Goodwin then made the point that Moyers and many others have made throughout the years: "The most important feature of this notorious spot was what it didn't say. Barry Goldwater's name was not mentioned. It was unnecessary. Everyone who saw it knew what it meant, and whom it meant."[73]

As Moyers correctly noted, Johnson was not the only candidate to attack his opponent that year. "Everyone remembers our campaign because of the Daisy Girl and the humor (sawing off the Eastern seaboard)," Moyers said, "but Goldwater struck first, with an ugly message in ads that attacked 'that mess in Washington.'" Indeed, one of the Goldwater spots used the words, "Graft . . . Swindle . . . Juvenile Delinquency . . . Crime . . . Riots. Hear what Barry Goldwater has to say about our lack of moral leadership." Then, Goldwater's voice: "The leadership of this nation has a clear and immediate challenge to go to work effectively and go to work immediately to restore proper respect for law and order in this land." In Johnson's defense, Moyers argued, "I can't blame LBJ for wanting to fight back against a candidate who was trying to paint the president of the United States as the head Vandal at the gates of Rome."[74] Ultimately, however, even Moyers, with forty-five years' perspective, regretted what Daisy Girl, and spots like it, wrought: "They appeal directly to the emotions, entering the body politic like heroin, enabling people to feel without thinking. On balance, I would un-invent them if it were possible."[75]

6 IN YOUR HEART, YOU KNOW HE MIGHT

Goldwater believed that Johnson and the DDB ads had severely damaged his candidacy. "There was no doubt as to the meaning [of the Daisy Girl spot]," he would write in 1988. "Barry Goldwater would blow up the world if he became President of the United States."[1] Adding to the indignity of the assault, the Daisy Girl spot, as earlier noted, never mentioned Goldwater by name—something that spoke volumes about the state of Goldwater's candidacy and the damage his various statements about nuclear weapons and nuclear war had already caused. "Goldwater was running not so much against Johnson as against himself—or the Barry Goldwater the image-makers had created," journalist Theodore White observed. "Rockefeller and Scranton had drawn up the indictment, Lyndon Johnson was the prosecutor. Goldwater was cast as defendant. He was like a dog with a can tied to his tail—the faster he ran, the more the can clattered."[2]

Trying to erase what White described as "the cartoon of himself," Goldwater went on the defensive and waged war on Johnson's terms. In a half-hour televised speech on September 18, Goldwater launched a vigorous defense of his candidacy in which he aided Johnson by violating that fundamental political law—never repeat your opponent's charge. In this and subsequent speeches, Goldwater noted that Johnson had called him "trigger-happy." Defending himself, the Republican candidate insisted that he wanted "peace through preparedness. The Republican Party is the party of peace—because we understand the requirements of peace, and because we understand the enemy." Communism, he said, was "the schoolyard bully" who, in the absence of a U.S. challenge, "eventually you'll have to fight."[3] The next day, in Buffalo, North Dakota, Goldwater sounded more bellicose, telling his audience at the National Plowing Contest that "today we are at war as certainly as the sun sets in the west." Calling for a challenge to Soviet Premier Khrushchev, Goldwater added, "If Communism intends to bury us, let us tell Communists loud and clear we're not going to hand them the shovel."[4]

A few days later, in Texas, Goldwater turned the debate back to an issue that had dogged him for months—his statements about whether the NATO commander should be given control of tactical nuclear weapons. Alleging that Johnson had already given such authority to NATO, Goldwater insisted that he was merely supporting the continuation of current policy. "There is real need for the supreme commander to be able to use judgment on the use of these weapons more expeditiously than he could by telephoning the White House," Goldwater said, "and I would say that in these cases the supreme commander should be given great leeway in the decision to use them or not to use them." Insisting that Johnson had already delegated such authority—a charge the Defense Department refused to confirm—Goldwater again repeated the charge against him: "If I can be called trigger-happy for suggesting it, what can you call the President for having already done it?"[5]*

Seeking to dispel the warmonger image, in late September Goldwater persuaded former president Eisenhower to sit down with him for a filmed interview in which the two men would address, head on, the charges against the Republican candidate. In an edited version shown on national television on September 22, Goldwater again repeated the charge, telling Eisenhower: "Our opponents are referring to us as warmongers, and I'd like to know what your opinion of that would be." A clearly uncomfortable Eisenhower responded, curtly, "Well, Barry, in my mind, this is actual tommyrot. Now, you've known about war; you've been through one. I'm older than you; I've been in more. But I'll tell you, no man that knows anything about war is going to be reckless about this."[6] In the thirty-minute national broadcast (also made into a one-minute spot), Eisenhower seemed to confirm the charge that Goldwater was the kind of person who would threaten the Soviets with war. "After all," he told Goldwater, "brinkmanship is absolutely necessary to keep the peace."[7]

Not only did Goldwater remain on the defensive, using Johnson's ver-

---

*Goldwater was likely correct. As historian Robert Dallek wrote in his biography of John F. Kennedy, Johnson's predecessor had learned to his dismay that the "command control" rules he inherited from Dwight D. Eisenhower allowed for "a subordinate commander faced with a substantial Russian military action [to] start the thermonuclear holocaust on his own initiative" (Robert Dallek, *An Unfinished Life: John F. Kennedy, 1917–1963* [Boston: Little, Brown, 2003], 344).

batim allegations in his speeches, he also persisted in using language that seemed designed to scare his audiences at a time when he should have been looking to speak in reassuring tones. In a bellicose October 1 speech in Hammond, Indiana, Goldwater uttered "holocaust, "push the button," and "finger is near that button." Each word or phrase, read in context, was not inherently problematic—but a candidate more careful with his rhetoric would surely have found a way to make the same points without employing language that reminded listeners of allegations about his recklessness. Absent that, the tone of Goldwater's speeches only grew more alarmist and militaristic. "We will not start a war against anyone," he said in the Hammond speech. "And the Communists must be certain that any holocaust they unleash will result in their own destruction and the end of their system."[8] Noting that Goldwater was defending himself against charges that he would start a nuclear war, Theodore White lamented that "the tone, and the foreign policy of immediate, uncompromising and aggressive challenge to the Soviet Union, could not but be reported with all their appropriate warlike and martial quotes."[9]

As long as Goldwater persisted in keeping alive the debate over who was better qualified to control the nation's nuclear arsenal, Johnson was more than willing to oblige. "In an age such as this," Johnson said in Baltimore in late October, "there would be no second chance for America's leadership to have second thoughts . . . If peace is to be preserved, America's voters, like America's leaders, must be right the first time or there will be no second time."[10]

Adding to Goldwater's woes was the fact that he was sorely misinformed about the nature of tactical nuclear weapons, which he seemed to believe were simply very powerful versions of field artillery. In August, speaking to the Veterans of Foreign Wars in Cleveland, Goldwater had referred to "these small, conventional nuclear weapons, which are no more powerful than the firepower you have faced on the battlefield. They simply come in a smaller package." As *Time* observed in its September 25 special edition devoted to nuclear weapons, "Goldwater shows appalling ignorance when he estimates that there are atomic weapons so small that they can be carried around by an infantryman, and [that] these weapons do not really have much more explosive power than some of the gunpowder arms of World War II." In fact, *Time* noted, the nation's smallest nuclear weapon, the Davy Crockett, "carries a minimum power package equivalent to 40 tons on TNT—as opposed to World War II's powerful 'blockbuster' bomb, which packed an explosive load of about 1½ tons."[11]

Goldwater's rhetoric prior to the campaign was perplexing enough. That he would double down on his bellicose language after Johnson had—very persuasively—implied that the Republican's election could result in a nuclear holocaust, is confounding. A headstrong man, Goldwater seemed unable to admit that his views on nuclear weapons were either uninformed or out of the mainstream of American political thought. It's not clear that Johnson's advisors knew that their advertising, combined with Goldwater's stubborn streak, would send the Republican nominee into an escalation of rhetoric about nuclear war; the result, however, was clearly everything they could have hoped for—and more. In campaign speeches Goldwater spoke of "liberating Eastern Europe," "victory over Communism," ensuring that the United States possessed "devastating strike-back power," and "suicide for the Communists if they should ever push the button." If the Soviets did push the button, Goldwater vowed to "destroy them." One *New York Times* correspondent covering Goldwater's campaign reported that during one speech he stopped counting after the Republican senator uttered such words and phrases as "holocaust," "push the button," and "atomic weapons" thirty times. "Thus," observed historian Melyvn H. Bloom, "there seemed always to be a threat, a willingness to gamble with human lives, inherent in Goldwater's comments on national defense."[12] In fact, based on his rhetorical behavior *after* the Daisy Girl spot aired, it would have been almost impossible not to take Goldwater at his word when he said, many years later, "I didn't want to run for the presidency. That's God's truth."[13]

By his own admission, Goldwater refused the advice of advisors and consultants who wanted to make him more acceptable to the American voting public. "The pros never would have done it our way—putting the conservative cause before winning the nomination or the election," he wrote in 1988. "So who needed them? We weren't going to compromise." From the beginning of the campaign, Goldwater insisted, he had decided not to trim his sails. "For better or worse, I would be myself—a straight-shooting, down-the-line conservative—for the entire campaign."[14]

In her analysis of the race, media scholar Kathleen Hall Jamieson observed, "If ever there was a campaign in which one candidate sought to win the election while the other was more interested in winning the point," the 1964 presidential campaign "was that contest." In most presidential contests of the past fifty years, the major party nominees have devoted their efforts in the general election campaign to winning over independent, or swing, voters who might have been alienated during the primaries. Struggles for major party nominations often force candidates, as they pursue the support of interest groups, to stake out positions farther to the left or right than the independent voters who usually decide most elections. Thus, once their nomination and the support of these interest groups are secure, the nominees are free to begin moving toward the middle of the ideological spectrum. It is in the ideological middle where most modern presidential campaigns have been waged. Johnson's behavior and rhetoric, for example, were typical of major-party presidential candidates during most general election periods. His messages were clearly aimed at persuading independent voters that he was a moderate, peace-loving, trustworthy, and measured leader. Goldwater was a different story. As Jamieson noted, "his final position was not further to the center by the election's end." Goldwater, Jamieson wrote, attempted during the general election period to "move the vast majority of the middle to where *he* stood rather than attempting to present his philosophy in terms palatable to the moderate middle."[15]

In his history of the campaign, Theodore White likened Goldwater's experience to having "a heavy mattress" thrown over him, "and he lay buried under it, trying to wriggle his way out." If Goldwater spent the latter months of the campaign being smothered, it was only partly Johnson's doing. The weighty mattress of fear and uncertainty may have made it difficult for Goldwater to get his campaign moving; that mattress, however, was largely one of Goldwater's own making. As White wrote elsewhere in his book, "no man ever began a Presidential effort more deeply wounded by his own nomination, suffering more insurmountable handicaps. And then it must be added that he made the worst of them."[16]

It did not help Goldwater's cause that many of the most influential voices in the national media were alarmed by the Republican candidate's increasingly bellicose rhetoric. For months, many reporters covering Goldwater's campaign had gone to great lengths to kindly interpret his most extreme statements. On the occasions when Goldwater uttered a particularly reckless or indiscrete remark, his press coterie often helped him walk back his remarks by asking for clarification. "Most reporters are personally fond of him," *Time* said in a July 24 story. At one point during the summer, that fondness saved Goldwater from grave embarrassment. Letting down his guard during an informal but on-the-record conversation with reporters, Goldwater suggested that the military challenge in Vietnam could be solved by striking China with nuclear weapons. When the stunned reporters asked if he really meant what he had said, the candidate thought better of the remark, retracted it, and the reporters did not quote him.[17] It was, it appeared, difficult for many reporters to believe that a U.S. senator could hold some of the views that Goldwater professed. Recalling many of the intemperate and confusing comments Goldwater had made earlier in the campaign, White presumably spoke for many of his journalist colleagues when he mused, "How could one be fair to Goldwater—by quoting what he said or by explaining what he thought? To quote him directly was manifestly unfair, but if he insisted on speaking thus in public, how could one resist quoting him?"[18]

Even when criticizing or mocking Johnson's message of fear, some in the media appeared to do Goldwater more harm than good. Writing in the *Indianapolis Star* in late September, columnist Don Campbell chided Johnson for "reducing questions and their answers to the lowest common denominator." The Johnson campaign seemed "slanted toward the nation's five-year-olds," wrote Campbell, who then helpfully summarized Johnson's message for his readers: "Here is Mr. Goldwater. He is a bad man. He would blow up little girls who pick daisies in his yard."[19]

Campbell's characterization of the Daisy Girl spot pointed to a common misunderstanding that simultaneously hurt Goldwater and shielded Johnson and DDB from the harshest criticism of their advertising approach. "Many people, especially the Republicans, shouted that the spot accused Senator Goldwater of being trigger-happy," Tony Schwartz recalled in his 1973 book, *The Responsive Chord*. "But *nowhere in the spot is Goldwater mentioned*. There is not even an indirect reference to Goldwater." As Schwartz noted, a modern-day viewer, with no historical background in the politics of 1964, could watch the Daisy Girl spot and never think of Goldwater. So, why the profound connection to him? "The commercial," Schwartz believed, "*evoked* a deep feeling in many people that Goldwater might actually use nuclear weapons. This mistrust was not in the *Daisy* spot. It was in the people who viewed the commercial. The stimuli of the film and sound evoked these feelings and allowed people to express what they inherently believed. Even today [1973], when people try to remember the *Daisy* spot, they recall their feelings, not the actual content of the commercial."[20]

As evidence, Schwartz cited a May 22, 1972, *New York Times* story in which reporter Ted Venetoulis incorrectly described the Daisy Girl spot: "Sometimes a candidate need not appear on the screen. In 1964, the Democrats demolished Goldwater with a simple one-shot television spot. A little girl gently picking daisies moved happily across an open field. Suddenly, a mushroom cloud filled the air and the announcer asked sternly, 'Whose finger do you want on the trigger?'"[21] Venetoulis's memory failed him. The girl remained in place; the mushroom cloud did not appear suddenly, but instead after the close-up of the girl's eye and the countdown; and, the announcer said nothing about a finger, nor a trigger, but rather, "Vote for President Johnson on November 3rd. The stakes are too high for you to stay home."[22]

Schwartz later recounted a conversation he had in the mid-1970s with F. Clifton White, one of Goldwater's campaign aides, who reported that

> very intelligent people would say to me: "We just cannot use atomic weapons." And I would then say to them, "Well, now, do you know what the Senator has said?" "Yeah, he said he would use atomic weapons." And I'd say, "No, he didn't say he would use an atomic bomb. He did say that one of the weapons we *could* use in Vietnam was a tactical nuclear weapon for defoliating the forests. A tactical nuclear weapon is like a small bomb, not a big one . . . Its purpose is to defoliate, to take the leaves off, so that we could see them down there." But all the time I'm going through this explanation, the person is standing there, nodding his head, and saying, "Yeah, but we can't drop the bomb, Clif." It was so totally emotional.[23]

Even someone as sophisticated as the advertising icon Rosser Reeves, who produced Dwight Eisenhower's groundbreaking television spots in 1952, thought he saw Goldwater in the spot. In an interview for a 1984 book about political advertising, Reeves told the authors that he remembered seeing a mushroom cloud emerging from Goldwater's head.[24]

Adding to the doubts about Goldwater's candidacy was the publication in September of a "special issue" of *Fact,* a bimonthly magazine published by radical journalist Ralph Ginzburg. The magazine featured a lengthy examination of Goldwater's temperament and mental state in which Ginzburg concluded: "This is a man who obviously identifies with a masculine mother rather than an effeminate father, and is victim to all the ambivalence that such identification must create. He must aggressively prove every moment of his life that he is a man . . . and in his irrationally cruel and spiteful pranks he manifests all the hostility that such ambivalence creates. But the seriousness of his malady, the extent of which it dominates his thinking and the danger it represents, are best revealed in the field of politics."[25]

In a separate article by Warren Boroson, *Fact* published the results of its poll of psychiatrists who provided answers to the question, "Do you believe Barry Goldwater is psychologically fit to serve as President of the United States?" Out of 12,356 psychiatrists who reportedly received the survey, only 2,417 responded. Of those—none of whom had actually examined Goldwater—1,189 said they believed the Republican was psychologically unfit to be president. A Los Angeles physician noted Goldwater's "impulsive, impetuous behavior," which, he wrote, "could result in world destruction." A doctor from New York wrote, "The public speeches and statements of Senator Goldwater suggest to me excessive aggressiveness in a dangerous nuclear context. Some aggression is normal. Some aggression is psychopathic." Among those expressing worries about Goldwater starting a nuclear war was the medical director of a New York psychiatric center. "We can survive almost all other mistakes that an unstable President might make but [nuclear war] is what really causes me to be concerned about Goldwater's stability." A Cincinnati psychiatrist wrote, "I am highly fearful of Senator Goldwater's casually precipitating us into an all-out atomic war. His public utterances strongly suggest the megalomania of a paranoid personality."

The comments to *Fact,* however, were not all negative. "Your questionnaire cannot really be answered," one doctor wrote, "because whatever psychopathology Goldwater may have is not that overt that one can make a diagnosis by merely observing him on TV or reading what he writes." Among the more prescient and pungent responses was from a New Orleans psychiatrist who responded, "Goldwater is not psychologically fit to be President, but neither is Johnson. It is certain that we will have an immature, unstable, exhibitionistic, unpredictable, and probably dangerous man for President for the next four years."[26]

After the campaign, Goldwater sued Ginzburg for libel and in 1969 won a judgment of $75,000 in punitive damages—a decision upheld on appeal.[27] Despite that ultimate vindication, the weight of the *Fact* articles and other media commentary did their damage. The DDB advertising campaign and its various subtle and overt references to Goldwater's perceived cavalier attitude toward war, in general, and nuclear weapons, in particular, influenced public perceptions of the Republican candidate. A majority or significant plurality of voters surveyed in mid-September by the Louis Harris organization agreed with the statement that "Goldwater is for . . . going to war over Cuba" (71 percent); "use of the atom bomb in Asia" (58 percent); and "get[ing the] U.S. into [a] big war" (49 percent).[28] More than a month later, after many of the DDB ads had aired, the image of Goldwater as a reckless warmonger seemed burned into the psyche of a large percentage of voters. In another Louis Harris poll of likely voters, 58 percent agreed that Goldwater "acts before thinking things through." Another 51 percent said they believed Goldwater "would get America into a war," and 45 percent agreed with the statement "he's a radical."[29] In another Harris poll a week later, 57 percent of voters surveyed said they believed Goldwater would drop an atomic bomb in Asia.[30]

Those numbers comported with a Gallup poll published in late October in which, by a margin of 45 percent to 22 percent, voters said that Democrats "would be more likely to keep the United States out of World War III."[31] Meanwhile, Johnson's image as a peacemaker soared. Concerning the president, 70 percent of voters in a Harris poll published in mid-October said that he would do a better job than Goldwater of keeping the United States out of war and 68 percent believed he would do better at keeping world peace.[32]

Those views of Goldwater were often echoed and amplified in the pages of major newspapers and news magazines. Fear of a Goldwater presidency among the media elite was a potent and growing force in the summer and fall of 1964. "It has become clear that [Goldwater] is not a normal American politician who, as election approaches, is drawn toward the center," respected columnist Walter Lippmann wrote in *Newsweek* in early July. "He is a radical agitator who must stay with the extremists." Goldwater's nomination represented "a grave threat to the internal peace of the nation," Lippmann insisted, adding that even his nomination "would be a national calamity."[33] Days before the Republican National Convention, in July, James Reston, the Washington bureau chief for the *New York Times*, wrote a scathing column in which he lamented that a President Goldwater would have the power to invade Cuba, break diplomatic relations with the Soviets or intervene in Eastern Europe. More alarming to Reston was Goldwater's stated desire "to hand over tactical nuclear weapons to the NATO commander for use on the commander's own authority in an emergency."

These are not casual proposals. Nothing is more certain in this uncertain world than that such a policy would have precisely the opposite effect from what the Senator desires. He offers to lead and strengthen the NATO alliance on this basis, but he would shatter it . . . It is a remarkable situation: for here is the party of "respectability," of "responsibility," of "equality," and of "peace" handing leadership in a cold war and a racial revolution to a militant man who want to leave war to the soldiers, and the Negro to the states. [The Republicans] are giving us a choice in San Francisco all right, but what a choice![34]

As the Republican National Convention gathered, columnist Drew Pearson wrote that "the smell of fascism has been in the air at this convention." Following the convention, the press criticism of Goldwater's intemperance intensified. "It is unfortunate that Goldwater is saddled with iron-clad opinions," nationally syndicated columnist Jim Bishop wrote, "and has the reaction time of a rattlesnake with a toothache."[35] By October, the doubts about Goldwater, stoked so well by Johnson's rhetoric and DDB's advertising, resulted in a crescendo of editorial support for Johnson. In mid-October, the results of a survey by *Editor and Publisher* revealed that of the 572 daily newspapers endorsing a presidential candidate, 300 had endorsed Johnson. *Editor and Publisher* reported that for the first time since its survey began in 1932, a majority of U.S. daily newspapers—many traditionally owned by conservative Republican businessmen—were supporting a Democrat for president. More impressive was that the papers endorsing Johnson represented 19.8 million subscribers versus the 6.2 million subscribers for those papers backing Goldwater.[36]

Among the media organizations backing Johnson was *Life* magazine, owned by Time, Inc., founder Henry Luce. It was the first time Luce or any of his influential publications had endorsed a Democratic presidential candidate. While *Life*'s sister publication *Time* did not endorse a candidate, several of its columnists, most prominently Lippmann, were openly hostile to Goldwater. The magazine's editors may also have been signaling their sentiments in the September 18 edition when they prominently published this riddle—based on the Daisy Girl spot—as told in a Greenwich Village stage production: "Goldwater's first major address as President will begin as follows: 'Ten . . . nine . . . eight . . . seven . . . six . . . five . . . four . . .' To anyone who might wonder what life would be like under President Goldwater, the answer is: 'Brief.'"[37]

The staid, conservative *Saturday Evening Post*—which had endorsed Richard Nixon, Dwight D. Eisenhower, Thomas Dewey, Herbert Hoover, and Calvin Coolidge—published a strongly worded editorial under the headline, "Why Lyndon Johnson Must Be Re-elected." Of Goldwater, the magazine said, "[his] tongue is like quicksilver; his mind like quicksand . . . [he] changes 'convictions' almost as often as his shirt . . . a grotesque burlesque of the conservative he pretends to be. He is a wild man, a stray, an unprincipled and ruthless political jujitsu artist like Joe McCarthy."[38] Among papers backing Johnson was the *Miami News*, which said in its September 22 editorial: "America does not need as its President a man who . . . would argue that the smaller nuclear weapons are nothing more than large conventional weapons."[39] Even Goldwater's home-state newspapers, the *Arizona Republic* (owned by longtime Goldwater patron Eugene Pulliam) and the *Phoenix Gazette* endorsed Johnson.[40]

In mid-October, fate and international events intervened in a way that only served to highlight the importance of electing a steady and rational president. On October 14, Kremlin leaders deposed Soviet leader Nikita Khrushchev, replacing him with Leonid Brezhnev. Two days later, the Chinese government exploded its first nuclear device at Lop Nor, in the country's Xinjiang desert. On October 18, two weeks before the November 3 election, Johnson delivered a prime-time network television speech in which he addressed the potential dangers of the two events and sought to portray himself as a sober, wise leader during times of international turmoil. Describing his meeting with the Soviet ambassador to the United States, Johnson said, "I told him that we intend to bury no one, and we do not intend to be buried." Of the Chinese nuclear test, Johnson warned that "no American should treat this matter lightly," adding that the testing of nuclear weapons "pollute[s] the atmosphere with fallout." Affirming his continued support for the nuclear test ban treaty (which Goldwater opposed), Johnson asserted "that we are right to recognize the danger of nuclear spread; that we must continue to work against it, and we will."[41]

As Election Day approached, Goldwater's reputation as a radical and warmonger was firmly planted in the minds of a majority of Americans— and many in the news media. Johnson, who could taste a landslide that would legitimize his presidency, turned up his attacks on Goldwater's perceived radicalism—and used some of Goldwater's words from his convention speech to do it. "Extremism in the pursuit of the presidency is an unpardonable vice," Johnson told those gathered a rally in New York City the evening before the election. "Moderation in the affairs of the nation is the highest virtue."[42]

While they did not recognize the need for a modern and effective advertising campaign, such as the one DDB had designed for Johnson, Goldwater's campaign had no plan to simply absorb the attacks without a response. Goldwater's television advertising strategy had been based primarily on producing longer, five-minute and thirty-minute television programs, which the campaign ran during prime time on one of the three networks. The problem was that the shows were poorly produced and not compelling. Whenever a Goldwater program appeared, many viewers quickly abandoned it for more entertaining fare on another network. As in past Republican presidential campaigns, Goldwater's advisors relied heavily on radio programs broadcast in local markets, as well as on national networks. From October 28 to election eve, for example, the Republican nominee broadcast a nightly five-minute radio "Goldwater Report" on the three hundred stations of the Mutual Broadcasting System.[43]

That strategy a failure, by October Goldwater's advisors cast about for a new approach. Instead of producing sixty-second spots that viewers might actually watch, they opted for more arresting and better-produced thirty-minute films that would, they hoped, take the spotlight off their candidate's bellicose rhetoric and instead stoke fears of a full presidential term for Johnson. The program, called "Choice," juxtaposed disturbing images of sexual promiscuity, moral bankruptcy, and racial unrest (representing Johnson's America) with tranquil, traditional, patriotic scenes (representing Goldwater's America). Interjected between jarring images of lewd dancing, female strippers, rioting, and gambling was a black Lincoln speeding recklessly along a dirt road. In one scene, the driver tosses a beer can from the car. That image was meant to associate Johnson— reported to occasionally drive his own Lincoln at high speeds on his sprawling Texas ranch while drinking beer—with the disturbing scenes of moral corruption. In a memorandum to campaign advisors, Goldwater's publicity director explained that "the purpose of this film is to portray and remind people of something they already know exists, and that is the moral crisis in America . . . We just wanted to make them mad, make their stomachs turn."[44]

Early in the film, the narrator, actor Raymond Massey, intoned, "Now there are two Americas. One is words like 'allegiance' and 'Republic.' This America is an ideal, a dream. The other America is no longer a dream, but a nightmare. Our streets are not safe. Immorality begins to flourish. Violence pits American against American. We don't want this."[45]

Goldwater had approved the program's creation but was never involved in its production. Finally completed by the Los Angeles advertising firm of Anderson, Morgan, DeSantis and Ball at a cost of $50,000, the program was booked to air on NBC at 2 P.M. on October 22. That plan quickly collapsed when advisors showed the film to Goldwater. "It's nothing but a racist film," he scoffed and ordered its cancellation. While the film never aired on national television, the campaign nonetheless sent copies of "Choice" to Goldwater supporters around the country. Thousands of viewers saw it in private screenings at movie houses and drive-in theaters.[46]

Meanwhile, Goldwater continued mostly to rely on longer programs that few viewers watched. The campaign did, however, produce some sixty-second spots. Most were bland and featured Goldwater speaking in various settings. One, in particular, seemed designed to present a tamer, less disturbing version of "Choice." After screen shots of the words "Graft," "Swindles," "Juvenile Delinquency," "Crime," and "Riots," a male narrator introduced Goldwater, who was seated at a desk: "The leadership of this nation has a clear and immediate challenge to go to work effectively and go to work immediately to restore proper respect for law and order in this land—and not just prior to election day either," Goldwater said. "America's greatness is the greatness of her people, and let this generation, then, make a new mark for that greatness. Let this generation of Americans set a standard of responsibility that will inspire the world." Just as the Daisy Girl ad never named Goldwater, this spot never mentioned or pictured Johnson.[47]

Another sixty-second Goldwater spot aired late in the campaign featured actor Ronald Reagan, who defended the Republican nominee against charges of recklessness. "I've known Barry Goldwater for a long time," Reagan said, adding

> And when I hear people say he's impulsive and such nonsense, I boil over. Believe me, if it weren't for Barry keeping those boys in Washington on their toes, do you honestly think our national defense would be as strong as it is? And remember, when Barry talks about the way

to keep the peace, when he says that only the strong can remain free, he knows what he's talking about. And I know the wonderful Goldwater family. Do you honestly believe that Barry wants his sons and daughters involved in a war? Do you think he wants his wife to be a wartime mother? Of course not.[48]

On October 27, Reagan also delivered a thirty-minute nationally televised speech on behalf of Goldwater, "A Time for Choosing," in which he argued for Goldwater's candidacy, employing phrases and themes he would rely upon for the next sixteen years, until his own election as president in 1980. Some called the Reagan program the highlight of a dismal Goldwater campaign, but like the other advertisements, long or brief, it also appeared to have little impact—other than to launch Reagan's own political career.[49]

While Goldwater's staff and the RNC vigorously protested the Daisy Girl spot in the news media, they never addressed it directly in a television advertisement. The only direct reference about the spot in any paid Goldwater advertising appeared to be in a newspaper ad in the *Los Angeles Times* on November 1: "Why did Lyndon Johnson's campaign sponsor a television commercial showing a little girl being destroyed by a nuclear blast as she pulls petals from a daisy? Why do they use terror on television? Why are they planting fear?"[50]

Johnson won the election in a landslide, earning 61 percent of the vote to Goldwater's 38.5 percent. In addition to his home state of Arizona, Goldwater carried only Louisiana, Mississippi, Alabama, Georgia, and South Carolina. It was the most lopsided victory in a presidential election since Franklin Roosevelt's 1936 reelection and a masterful evisceration of Goldwater by Johnson. From the beginning, Johnson's team had resolved to paint its opponent as a dangerous radical—and the tactics rarely wavered. Goldwater "was treated, not as the leader of the Republican party," political scientist Stanley Kelley Jr. wrote in a 1966 book on the election, "but as the head of an extremist faction that had captured the Republican party." Kelley agreed with the *Washington Post*'s portrayal: Johnson cast Goldwater as "the spokesman of a fraction of a faction of reaction."[51] While some may have believed the election was a referendum on war (despite running as a peacemaker, Johnson would soon drastically escalate U.S. military's involvement in Vietnam), Theodore White dismissed that notion. It was never "a choice between war and peace," he insisted. "But it *was* a choice, nonetheless—between peace and *risk* of war." White recalled that Johnson's backers had answered Goldwater's slogan, "In Your Heart You Know He's Right," with this rejoinder: "In Your Heart, You Know He Might." That catchphrase seemed to sum up all the public's fears and doubts about Goldwater, aided by DDB and a little girl plucking flower petals. By the election, White wrote, "because they had been persuaded that indeed [Goldwater] *might*, millions of Americans voted against the Republicans."[52]

On the final day of the general election campaign, Goldwater had flown to San Francisco for a rally. He told the languid crowd that the campaign had not changed him. He was giving them the same speech with which he had launched his campaign. "The issues have not changed," he said. "I have not changed. The challenge and the choice has not changed."[53]

Assessing the campaign in the early 1970s for the multivolume *History of American Presidential Elections*, John Bartlow Martin begged to disagree. Everything had changed, he observed. "The issues—victory, big government, morality—which had sounded so good a year or so ago in the locker room of the Camelback Inn in Arizona [where Goldwater had begun his presidential campaign] had not sounded nearly so good on national television," Martin wrote. "Goldwater himself may not have changed but the kind of campaign he had been obliged to make—and which had been made for him—had certainly changed. As for the challenge and the choice, the challenge had hardly been made, the choice hardly presented. It was all rather sad."[54]

What Martin did not realize at the time was that, although Goldwater was indeed a profoundly imperfect candidate, the character of the decades-long struggle within the Republican Party between its moderate-to-liberal East Coast internationalist wing and its staunchly conservative Midwest and Western wing was changing. While they had lost the election, the conservatives were on the rise, an ascent that would culminate in the election of President Ronald Reagan in 1980 and the conservative revolution of subsequent decades.

For now, however, Goldwater's defeat was overwhelming and complete. Johnson smothered him in a landslide of unprecedented proportions, the result of a skillful campaign that earned the president a winning margin of almost 16 million votes. How did Johnson do it? Had his campaign destroyed Goldwater with a deadly fusillade of negative television spots and clever attacks in speeches and other media appearances?

Did Goldwater's chances (if he ever had any) vanish after Johnson un-leashed the Daisy Girl spot and other DDB creations that exploited Amer-icans' fears about the bomb and nuclear war?

These questions, of course, are impossible to answer conclusively. The evidence, however, suggests that instead of destroying Goldwater's slim chances for the White House, Johnson's plan to brand his opponent as a reckless extremist was substantially accomplished by Goldwater him-self. If Goldwater was the potter of his image, spinning his public per-sona into the shape of a bellicose radical, Johnson's campaign and the DDB spots merely served as the kiln, baking that image into something hard and durable.

But there was something more important—and more deadly to Gold-water—that DDB's spots may have accomplished. In books, statements, and speeches over several years, Goldwater had indeed crafted his own image. By the time he won the Republican nomination in July 1964, how-ever, the question was not whether Johnson could persuade a substantial portion of the electorate that his rival from Arizona was an extremist. *Rather, it was whether Johnson could demonstrate why a President Goldwa-ter's extremism would be a threat to world peace.* In January 1964, long be-fore Goldwater was a household name, Gallup asked American voters, "Which political party do you think should be more likely to keep the United States out of World War III"? Democrats prevailed by 34 percent to 21 percent—a 13-point margin. In the same poll, however, 44 percent of respondents said "same" (31 percent) or had no opinion (13 percent). How-ever, by late August—after Goldwater won the nomination but *before* the Daisy Girl and other DDB spots were aired—it was clear that public opin-ion had already shifted against Goldwater and his party. Asked the same question, voters now said, by 44 percent to 20 percent, that the Demo-crats would do better at preventing a world war—a ten-point increase in favor of the Democrats since January. The percentage who said "same" dropped from 31 to 20 percent. The two-to-one percentage of those who believed the Democrats would do better at preventing a world war re-mained fairly constant throughout the campaign (except for a brief spike to 54 percent in confidence for the Democrats in late August).[55]

The DDB spots which began in early September did, however, appear to have an impact—and it involved introducing fear into the campaign. In early September, Gallup asked voters, "What are your fears and wor-ries about the future? In other words, if you imagine your future in the worst possible light, what would your life look like then?" Twenty-nine percent answered "nuclear war, living in fear of war."[56] Asked the same question a month later, after many of the DDB ads had aired, Gallup's poll produced markedly different numbers. Fifty-one percent of those polled in early October expressed a fear of war, *more than twenty percentage points higher than a month before.*[57]

These polling data suggest that Goldwater's rhetoric had already persuaded voters that if war erupted it would be more likely under a Republican presidency. By early September, however, it does not appear that a significant percentage of voters actually *feared* that a nuclear war was *likely* under a potential Goldwater presidency. The DDB spots in September seem to have changed that by solidifying and amplifying existing perceptions about Goldwater—but more so by greatly enhancing existing fears about a potential Goldwater presidency. For example, in answer to another question in October 1964—*after* the DDB spots ran—voters now seemed to express greater concerns about the possibility of a world war should Goldwater enter the White House. Asked "how much trust and confidence you would have in the way Barry Goldwater . . . would handle . . . preventing World War III," 48 percent of respondents said "not very much" or "none at all." Only 12 percent expressed a "very great deal" of confidence in Goldwater.[58] In another poll in October, this one conducted by Louis Harris and Associates, 51 percent of respondents agreed with the statement, "Barry Goldwater would get America into a war."[59]

The question remains: Did the DDB spots, especially the Daisy Girl spot, destroy Goldwater's campaign? That is a difficult case to make. Public opinion surveys before and after the election indicate that instead of knocking out Goldwater, Johnson's campaign—including DDB's advertising—may have kept him pinned to the mat, unable to rise to fight, during the critical post–Labor Day campaign period. To say that DDB's spots knocked out Goldwater would be to argue that he was ever actually standing and in the fight. The polling data suggest that he was not. While the final margin of victory was narrower than polls taken in late 1963 might have indicated, Goldwater's poor campaign organization, his image as a radical, and his unfortunate rhetorical blunders never allowed him to get a full hearing from the vast majority of American voters.

A Gallup poll conducted in mid-December 1963, long before the Arizona senator won the Republican nomination, showed Johnson leading Goldwater, 75 percent to 20 percent, in a potential matchup. From

January 1964 through much of June, Johnson's support in the monthly Gallup poll never dipped below 73 percent; Goldwater's support during the same period never rose above 20 percent. Harris Survey polls during the same period showed greater support for Goldwater. In Harris polls, Goldwater was consistently in the mid-twenties and then, after the July Republican convention, in the low-to-mid thirties.

The Republican National Convention, held July 13 through 16, and the national attention it brought, gave Goldwater a significant boost and trimmed Johnson's support considerably. Gallup's poll conducted a week after the Republican convention showed the race narrowing—54 percent for Johnson to Goldwater's 26 percent. The improvement in Goldwater's numbers, however, was only temporary. By the next Gallup survey in early August, Johnson's support had recovered, back up to 63 percent; Goldwater's support had dropped slightly to 24 percent. Harris put the race, postconvention, at 64 to 36 percent. For the rest of the campaign, Gallup's numbers for Johnson and Goldwater moved only slightly. Most significant is that the Daisy Girl spot and the other DDB ads, which began airing on September 7, did not appear to affect Johnson's or Goldwater's poll numbers in either Harris or Gallup polls. In a Gallup poll conducted in late August, Johnson led Goldwater 68 to 26 percent. In another Gallup survey conducted September 18–23, in the midst of the barrage of DDB spots, the numbers had changed little. Johnson led Goldwater 67 to 29 percent—a three-point increase for Goldwater. Before the Daisy Girl spot, Harris reported Goldwater's support at 32 percent—the exact percentage he garnered in a poll after the Daisy Girl spot aired. His support in the October Gallup poll remained constant at 29 percent. In the Harris poll, he moved up two points to 34 percent.[60] On Election Day, Goldwater, as is typical of many challengers, appeared to get the vast majority of the undecided vote, which increased his final percentage to 38.5 percent.

"The Goldwater 'image' was indeed phenomenally unfavorable," public opinion scholars Philip E. Converse, Aage R. Clausen, and Warren E. Miller wrote in a lengthy analysis of the election in 1965. "Typically, American voters have tended on balance to speak favorably, even about candidates they were about to send down to defeat." Before 1964, the scholars noted, the least favorable image among presidential candidates was owned by Adlai Stevenson in 1956—only 52 percent of those polled had a favorable view of Eisenhower's Democratic challenger. In

Gallup and Harris Polls Presidential Trial Heats, December 1963–November 1964

Pollster	Polling Period	Johnson	Goldwater
Gallup	Dec. 12–17	75	20
Gallup	Jan. 2–7	73	19
Harris	Feb. 17	64	26
Gallup	March 13–17	78	13
Harris	April 6	66	26
Gallup	April 24–29	77	16
Gallup	May 6–11	76	16
Gallup	June 25-30	75	19
Harris	July 10	74	26
Harris	July 22*	64	36
Gallup	July 23–28*	54	26
Gallup	Aug. 6–11	63	24
Harris	Aug. 14	59	32
Gallup	Aug. 27–Sept. 1**	68	26
Harris	Sept. 2	59	32
Harris	Sept. 21***	60	32
Gallup	Sept. 18–23***	67	29
Gallup	Oct. 8–13	64	29
Harris	Oct. 12	58	34
Gallup	Oct. 25–30	64	29
Harris	Oct. 23	57	29
Harris	Nov. 2	62	33
Election Results	Nov. 3	61	38

Note: Harris surveys indicate date of publication, not polling period.

*Poll conducted immediately after GOP convention.
**Poll conducted after Democratic convention.
***Poll conducted after Sept. 7 broadcast of Daisy Girl spot.

Sources: George H. Gallup, *The Gallup Poll: Public Opinion, 1935–1971,* Vol. 3 (New York: Random House, 1972); Harris Survey results published in the *Washington Post.*

1964, according to Converse and his colleagues, less than 35 percent of references to Goldwater were favorable.[61]

While Democrats greatly outnumbered Republicans in the United States in 1964, Goldwater's unpopularity cannot be attributed only to the ideological leanings of voters. In a postelection survey in November 1964, Gallup asked voters which they would choose if there were only two major parties in the United States, "one for liberals and one for conservatives." Slightly more voters—37 percent to 35 percent—chose the conservative party.[62] An October Gallup survey revealed a similar, if more complex, division among voters, but certainly no liberal majority. Twenty-six percent of respondents called themselves conservative, 28 percent liberal, and 37 percent "middle of the road."[63] The numbers suggest that it was not conservatism that voters had rejected but rather Goldwater himself and his perceived extremism.

Further complicating matters for Goldwater was voters' attitudes toward his foreign policy positions. In 1956, voters told pollsters that Republicans could better handle foreign policy—40 percent to 7 percent. Four years later, when Richard Nixon and John F. Kennedy vied for the White House, the gap narrowed—29 to 15 percent—but still favored the Republicans. Goldwater's candidacy obliterated the Republican advantage in foreign policy. By 1964, voters trusted Democrats more than Republicans by 38 to 12 percent, a breathtaking reversal from only eight years earlier. "Thus to the many ways of describing the public's repudiation of the Goldwater candidacy," Converse, Clausen, and Miller wrote, "another may be added: between a party of prosperity and peace, as against a party of depression and war, there is little room for hesitation."[64]

Any contention that the Daisy Girl and other DDB spots destroyed Goldwater's candidacy is almost certainly overstating their impact. That, however, does not mean that the Daisy Girl spot was not a pivotal and historic moment in American political history. It is certainly one of the most famous spots in American political history. It may also be the most important. Indeed, in the realm of presidential television spot advertising, Daisy Girl and its sisters, produced by DBB, were revolutionary.

CONCLUSION

Running against John F. Kennedy for the Democratic presidential nomination in West Virginia in 1960, Senator Hubert Humphrey came to the end of his campaign funds. The Minnesota Democrat struggled to maintain some kind of presence on television lest he be swept aside in the wake of his opponent's enormous advertising budget. Kennedy was reportedly spending tens of thousands of dollars on television advertising, far more than Humphrey could afford for his entire West Virginia campaign operation.

His campaign coffers empty, Humphrey wrote a personal check for $750 to purchase thirty minutes of statewide TV time the weekend before the election. As he watched a glum Humphrey sign the check, journalist Theodore White said he had the feeling the Minnesota senator was tapping the "family grocery fund—or the money earmarked to pay for the wedding of [Humphrey's] daughter who was to be married the week following the primary." White also realized that Humphrey's check would purchase only television time, not the broadcast's preparation and production. Humphrey's bankrupt campaign would make do with a bare set and a telephone with two lines. Seated at a desk with the phone before him, Humphrey would himself answer one of the two blinking lines and respond to the unscreened calls on live television. White, who acknowledged that he would normally find such a situation comic, could in this case only muster pity.

After fielding several routine calls, Humphrey found himself on the line with an elderly woman calling from some remote part of the West Virginia hills. Humphrey flinched as the ornery woman admonished in a raspy voice, "You git out! You git out of West Virginia, Mr. Humphrey!" Humphrey gamely attempted a reply, but the woman persisted. "You git out, you hear! You can't stand the Republicans gitting ahead of you! Why don't you git out?"

Humphrey briefly recovered during several more calls only to have the broadcast descend to even lower and more embarrassing depths near the end of the painfully long thirty minutes. Just as he had begun to answer a question from a caller, a telephone operator interrupted. "Clear the wires, please, clear the wires, this is an emergency!" Humphrey explained to the operator that he was conducting a live, statewide television call-in show. "Clear the wires, clear the wires at once, this is an emergency." White recalled that Humphrey, "his face blank and bedazzled, hung up, shaken." By that time, White observed, "the telethon lost all cohesion— proving nothing except that TV is no medium for a poor man."[1]

Even with the resources to match Kennedy dollar for dollar on television, there is no guarantee that Humphrey would have prevailed. Kennedy was youthful, vital, and extremely telegenic. He also was pouring enormous amounts of his family's wealth into mobilizing the voters of the small, rural state—deploying organizational resources that Humphrey did not have. Yet while his television presence was certainly greater than Humphrey's, and better produced, the quality of Kennedy's television advertising was, by the standards of 1964 and 1968, exceedingly poor. What passed for television advertising in 1960 was mostly speeches, interviews, or call-in programs shown to viewers in five-, fifteen-, or thirty-minute blocks of time.

There had been flashes of brilliance in political advertising in the 1950s. The fifteen-second spots that Rosser Reeves had produced for Dwight Eisenhower in 1952—"Eisenhower Answers America"—were groundbreaking and effective in communicating the retired general's unique selling propositions—his determination to win (or end) the Korean War, stop government corruption, and control inflation. Such creativity in political advertising was the exception, not the rule. Even Reeves acknowledged that his spots for Eisenhower rated fairly low on the artistic scale. "Unlike a lot of my competitors, I never tried to make *interesting* commercials," Reeves later said.[2] Shrill, hard-sell blandness and lack of creative vision largely ruled the political airwaves, even throughout the early 1960s, when advertising firms found creative ways to sell all manner of products, such as soap, cars, cigarettes, and cereal.

Typical of Kennedy's advertising during the general election was a one-minute spot in which the awkward-looking candidate, dressed in a dark suit, sat on a sofa in the living room of the "Sills family" and quizzed them about their economic struggles: "What's been your experience, Mr. Sills? How are you keeping those two daughters of yours going?"[3] In another spot, a chorus sang a Kennedy jingle—"Do you want a man for President who's seasoned through and through / but not so doggoned seasoned that he won't try something new?"—as an amateurish mix of still photographs and other graphics marched across the screen.[4] Nixon's spots were even less imaginative. Most of the Republican candidate's spots featured a stiff, unsmiling vice president seated on the edge of a desk as he talked to the camera.[5]

By the 1968 presidential election, however, political advertising had undergone a stunning transformation. Richard Nixon's and Hubert Humphrey's spots were mostly in color, featured creative uses of music and other sound, and employed imagery that demonstrated a fuller understanding of how to use television to generate emotional responses rather than simply dispense information. In a particularly moving spot designed to evoke fears about Nixon's supposed lack of concern for education and other social issues, Humphrey's media team showed a mother cuddling and singing to a baby. "He's so adorable," the mother says. "I wonder what it will be like when he's older. What's going to happen to him? I hope he won't be afraid the way we are. There's so much violence now. I wouldn't be so scared if I felt they understood what it's all about, and they cared." In another spot, Humphrey attempted a reprise of the Daisy Girl spot. Over footage of a nuclear explosion, the announcer asks, "Do you want Castro to have the bomb—now? Do you want any country that doesn't have the bomb to be able to get it?"[6]*

Nixon, who had appeared in unimaginative talking-head spots eight years before, aired a series of television commercials featuring an artistic use of still photographs, which he narrated. The spots showed no images of the candidate, except for a flattering portrait at the end. In one spot, over a series of photographs of children and babies, Nixon says, "I see the face of a child. What his color is, what his ancestry is, doesn't matter. What does matter is he's an American child. That child is more im-

*The Humphrey campaign had originally hired DDB to produce its campaign advertising but fired the firm over creative differences only six weeks before Election Day. The account went to Campaign Planners Associates, a group made up of executives from the large advertising firm of Lennen and Newell ("Making the Image," *Time*, Sept. 27, 1968; "The Political Pitch," *Newsweek*, Oct. 14, 1968).

portant than any politician's promise. He is everything we've ever hoped to be, and everything we dare to dream to be."[7]

While Nixon's and Humphrey's spots were light years removed from the crude and rudimentary spots created for their campaigns in 1960, Nixon's campaign proved to be more creative and appeared to better understand the power of television in politics. Internal memoranda gathered by author Joe McGinniss for his book about the 1968 Nixon campaign, *The Selling of the President,* demonstrate that the former vice president's media advisors understood the relative worth of issues versus the image and personality traits of the candidate. "Issues will be discussed," Harry Treleaven wrote in November 1967 to Nixon campaign aides, "but always in a way that clearly establishes Richard Nixon as the Republican candidate who is best equipped to deal with them." Another Nixon media advisor, William Gavin, assessed Senator Robert Kennedy's appeal and concluded that the key was "an emotional posture without bothering with a reasoned analysis. It's the emotion that gets across, the posture, the sense of involvement and concern." Gavin, in fact, cautioned against relying too much on reason.

> Reason requires a high degree of discipline, of concentration; impression is easier.
> Reason pushes the viewer back, it assaults him, it demands that he agree or disagree; impression can envelope him, invite him in, without making an intellectual demand, or a demand on his intellectual energies. He can receive the impression without having to think about it in a linear, structured way. When we argue with him we demand that he make the effort of replying. We seek to engage his intellect, and for most people this is the most difficult work of all. The emotions are more easily roused, closer to the surface, more malleable.
> Get the voters to like the guy, and the battle's two thirds won.[8]

Of using reasoned appeals in politics, Ray Price, another media advisor to Nixon, argued that the campaign should strive instead to persuade voters to take "the *emotional* leap" in which "we can make them *feel* that he's got the aura of a winner." None of that, Price and his colleagues believed, would be accomplished with reason. As Price observed, "The natural human use of reason is to support prejudices, not to arrive at opinions." Price emphasized this point. "It's not what's *there* that counts, it's what's projected—and, carrying it one step further, it's not what *he* projects but rather what the voter receives. It's not the man we have to change, but rather the *received impression*. And this impression often depends more on the medium and its use than it does on the candidate himself."[9]

In this sense, it is clear that in 1968 the men who developed Nixon's television advertising were almost perfectly in tune with the person who helped produce some of Humphrey's spots—Tony Schwartz, the man who had also helped create the Daisy Girl spot. "Television is an ideal medium for surfacing feelings voters already have," Schwartz wrote in his 1973 book, *The Responsive Chord*, "and giving these feelings a direction by providing stimuli that may evoke the desired behavior." To Schwartz, "The real question in political advertising is *how to surround the voter with the proper auditory and visual stimuli to evoke the reaction you want for him, i.e., his voting for a specific candidate* [emphasis Schwartz]."[10]

Schwartz argued that much of political advertising was tired and ineffective. "The 'image people' work with concepts like *charismatic, handsome, youthful,* etc.," he wrote. "And they strive to keep their candidate *moving*—through shopping centers, old-age homes, schools, etc." To these political advertisers, television was "a vehicle for bringing the voters to the candidate, where they can see and experience his glorious image." In Schwartz's world, the equation was reversed. "I believe it is far more important to understand and affect the inner feelings of a voter in relation to a political candidate than to package an image that voters tend not to believe anyway," he wrote. "It would be more correct to say that the goal of a media adviser is to tie up the voter and deliver him to the candidate. So it is really the *voter* who is packaged by the media, not the candidate."[11]

When making that observation, Schwartz undoubtedly had in mind the 1964 presidential campaign of Lyndon Johnson. Indeed, he devoted several pages to the Daisy Girl spot in the same chapter. Concluding his discussion of the spot, Schwartz emphasized a point he had made elsewhere in the book. "Commercials that attempt to *tell* the listener something are inherently not as effective as those that attach to something that is already in him," he wrote. "We are not concerned with getting things *across* to people as much as *out* of people."[12]

The fundamental conservative shift in American politics that began in 1964 would not become apparent until the late 1970s. More immediate, however, was that election's profound and lasting impact on the way presidential candidates, especially those running for the White House, used television spot advertising to influence voters. Examine any of the television spots created for presidential candidates in 1952, 1956, or 1960. Then, look at Barry Goldwater's spots from 1964. (This is easily accomplished by visiting the website "The Living Room Candidate.") Goldwater's spots appear frozen in time. Stylistically, there is little difference between the 1964 Goldwater spots and those produced more than a decade earlier. While Goldwater's campaign plowed almost 40 percent of its budget into television advertising—and, by one estimate, outspent Johnson on television by 40 percent—the Republican's commercials were mostly documentary films, speeches, and lengthy interviews. The candidate's advisors had rejected the counsel of their advertising agency—Erwin, Wasey, Ruthrauff, and Ryan—to employ shorter spot advertising.

Because of the unpopularity of this long-format style advertising, Goldwater's campaign may have been partly responsible for the huge success of the prime-time ABC drama "Peyton Place." Then-NBC president Robert Kintner suggested that Goldwater's decision to preempt his network's 9:30 to 10:00 P.M. time slot three times in October drove NBC's audience to ABC and gave the rival network's new show "its huge audience."[13] "You couldn't convince [the Goldwater campaign]," one advertising executive later complained, "that voters' favorite entertainment shows—like Petticoat Junction—shouldn't be preempted." As Joanne Morreale argued in her 1993 book, *The Presidential Campaign Film,* the "common lore" of the time "was that the advertisers knew nothing about politics, and the political operatives knew nothing about television. The Goldwater campaign was no exception."[14]

The Johnson campaign, however, was the exception. The contrast between Johnson's spots in 1964 and John F. Kennedy's in 1960 is remarkable. In style, the difference is more like a decade removed, not just four years. It was the creative executives at DDB in 1964 who helped show politicians how to use television not simply to inform but to *persuade.* And not so much to persuade viewers but to give them an *experience.* The DDB spots were a hinge in presidential campaign history. The Daisy Girl spot's skillful manipulation of the fears residing in American viewers showed a new generation of political professionals that television advertising in campaigns was about far more than which candidate had the best facts; it was, instead, more about which candidate could give meaning to the facts—and fears—the voters already possessed. Daisy Girl and the other spots produced for Johnson qualify as the first television spots of the *mod-*

ern political era—an era in which presidential candidates increasingly and effectively used emotion, not reason, to win elections.

■ ■ ■

In the years since the 1964 election, it is likely that no presidential campaign commercial has been viewed more than the Daisy Girl spot. Despite having been shown just a handful of times on national television—and only once as a paid advertisement—the spot was not only credited (inaccurately) for the historic defeat of Barry Goldwater but also ushered in a new era in political advertising in which the *chief objective* was emotion, not information. The spot and the others like it that DDB produced in the summer and fall of 1964 helped change American politics and political advertising in several other important ways:

1. Daisy Girl was the first spot to use the emotion of *fear* in American presidential campaigns, a tactic that would soon be widely used in political television advertising. To be sure, fear as a campaign tactic had been a staple of American politics since the founding of the Republic. A powerful force in any medium, the use of fear in dramatic televised form elevated—or lowered, depending on one's view—the practice to a new and particularly potent level.

The Daisy Girl spot was not, however, responsible for creating the fear it exploited. Instead, as Tony Schwartz has noted, it creatively harnessed the *existing* fear of nuclear war—a fact of American life for more than a decade—and put it to use as a weapon against Goldwater. Future candidates would emulate this tactic with varying degrees of effectiveness. In 1968, Richard Nixon's campaign would attempt to evoke fear and anger with a spot that suggested Hubert Humphrey was pleased by and would continue the carnage in Vietnam. In the same campaign, as previously noted, Humphrey used the imagery of a nuclear bomb to plant similar fears about Nixon. Ronald Reagan exploited fears of the Soviet Union in 1984 with his "Bear" spot, in which a bear roams through woods and over hills until it suddenly stops when it encounters a man with a gun. "Some say the bear is tame," the announcer stated, "others say it's vicious and dangerous." Four years later, George H. W. Bush and his supporters exploited fears of crime and racial tensions with spots about a prison furlough program in Massachusetts supported by his Democratic opponent, Gov. Michael Dukakis. One spot featured a group of swarthy, zombie-like men trudging through a turnstile. The announcer, over a sinister sound-track, attacked Dukakis's "revolving door prison policy [that] gave week-end furloughs to first-degree murderers not eligible for parole."[15]

2. The Daisy Girl spot may have been the most effective televised use of a narrative or story to convey a message in a presidential campaign. One scholar called it "issue dramatization," a technique used liberally in the 1952 presidential race by Eisenhower and Stevenson. The 1984 "Bear" and the 1988 prison furlough spots are also prominent examples of this. More than dramatization, however, the Daisy Girl spot may also have been the most successful use of symbolism in a presidential campaign spot. The peaceful scene in the field, with birds happily chirping, sym-bolized the idealized world threatened by Goldwater's election. The little girl represented the innocence at jeopardy in the election's outcome. She also symbolized an entire generation of young people whose futures were at risk. The daisy's falling petals symbolized the flower of youth being de-stroyed by the threat of nuclear war. The voice of the mission control an-nouncer, counting down toward the nuclear explosion, symbolized the space age gone awry—from peaceful exploration of the New Frontier to a new era in which nuclear bombs descending from the sky threatened the world's destruction. The violence of the explosion represented, liter-ally, the end of the world. The spot was "full of contrast and symbolism," cultural historian Paul Rutherford observed, "easy to understand, and packed with emotion. Above all, *Daisy* played out that role of the 'distil-lation': it had staged a display of the ultimate horror of those years, nu-clear holocaust."[16] "Facts aren't influential until they *mean* something to someone," Annette Simmons observes in her 2006 book *The Story Fac-tor.* "A story delivers context so that your facts slide into new slots in your listeners' brains."[17] So it was that the Daisy Girl and her story of nuclear annihilation gave meaning to the public's existing facts and fears con-cerning atomic war.

3. Daisy Girl was the first television spot in a presidential campaign that encouraged viewers to apply their own meaning by interpreting it through the prism of their own fears or experience. It was, as Tony Schwartz once described it, like "Rorschach patterns. They do not tell the viewer anything. They surface his feelings and provide a context for him to express those feelings."[18] The spot did not mention Goldwater by name; yet its clear message was that Goldwater's election would lead to nuclear war. Goldwater said it best in his memoir: "There was no doubt

as to the meaning: Barry Goldwater would blow up the world if he became President of the United States."[19] Put another way by communications scholar Scott Jacobs: "The salient qualities of this ad function primarily as a kind of framing device." Jacobs regarded the ad as "an especially clean example of a contribution of an argumentative activity where the contribution is designed to operate on *the conditions* for argumentation."[20] In other words, the ad put to use "the conditions"—Goldwater's reckless rhetoric about nuclear warfare—in a way that solidified the existing frame about Goldwater—a reckless man who might blow up the world—and encouraged viewers to explore and interpret information they already possessed to advance their own arguments against Goldwater.

4. It was the first presidential television spot designed to contain no real information and no rational argument (except for Johnson's inarguable statement at the end and the announcer's tag line, "The stakes are too high for you to stay home"). This is a major reason it was so effective: there was no charge or statement to dispute or with which to argue. The spot proved one of Neil Postman's major arguments in his seminal 1985 book on television, *Amusing Ourselves to Death:* "Whenever language is the principle medium of communication . . . an idea, a fact, a claim is the inevitable result." Postman further complains that "by substituting images for claims, the pictorial commercial made emotional appeal, not tests of truth, the basis of consumer decisions. The distance between rationality and advertising is now so wide that it is difficult to remember that there once existed a connection between them . . . No claims are made, except those the viewer projects onto or infers from the drama. One can like or dislike a television commercial, of course. But one cannot refute it."[21]

5. The spot was among the first to apply the *creative* principles of television advertising to presidential politics. Prior to 1964, a creative, groundbreaking spot was one that used cartoon animation or a campaign jingle or song. Most campaign spots were simply abbreviated or condensed campaign speeches. DBB brought to politics the same approach it applied to advertising automobiles, soap, and other products. In that way, Daisy Girl helped usher political advertising into the modern era.

6. The spot and its companions also represented a new and revolutionary mode of operation for the Democratic Party. In previous presidential campaigns, the Democratic Party had hired an advertising firm only to

produce spots that the candidate, his advisors, or the party's leaders devised. In other words, the advertising agencies were usually hired only for their technical production expertise. Johnson's advisors (and Kennedy's before him) wanted to hire DDB because they valued the firm as a creative force and recognized the enormous benefit of applying modern advertising principles and techniques to political campaigning. The results were revolutionary, and not just for the Democratic Party. The true innovation that transformed political advertising was not the campaign's decision to cede control of the creative content but rather its decision to demand that the content be creative.

7. Although not created for this purpose, Daisy Girl was the first political spot that garnered significant news media attention. It is likely that more viewers saw the spot replayed during the nightly networks' newscasts than actually saw it aired during "Monday Night at the Movies." Indeed, in a week's time, the spot may have been viewed by as many as 100 million people. By the 1980s, it would be a staple of political advertising to buy a small amount of airtime for a provocative or controversial spot in hopes of gaining significant "earned" media airplay. The inexpensive cable spots in 2004, in which the group "Swift Boat Veterans for Truth" attacked Democratic presidential candidate John Kerry's Vietnam War record, are a prime example.

While the Daisy Girl spot is widely regarded as effective, it is not so widely regarded as fair. At the time, Republican leaders filed official protests, charging that the spot violated basic decency standards. In his memoir, Goldwater devoted several pages to the spot, charging that it and other DDB commercials were the beginning of "electronic dirt" in politics. While researching the book, Goldwater reached out to several journalists to ask them for their opinions on the spot.

New York Times columnist James "Scotty" Reston told Goldwater, "I wish the media had kicked the stuffing out of LBJ and the White House on the TV ads issue. I think [Goldwater] is absolutely right in saying the press was remiss in letting that garbage get out without nailing them. It was outrageous—no doubt about it. He's got a legitimate gripe." (In 1964, Reston did not appear so outraged about Goldwater's treatment at the hands of Johnson and DDB. In a July 12 column, he asserted that Goldwater's election might shatter the NATO alliance.)[22] Then-*Washington Post* editor Ben Bradlee called the DDB bomb spots "a fucking outrage." The *Post*'s respected political writer David Broder told Goldwater that

Johnson's attacks on him were "highly irrational because they were so heavily favored to win. Also, the media's original perception of Goldwater was fundamentally false. He was not the crazy madman that some depicted." Broder, however, did acknowledge "some substantial criticism was justified," but added, "Our characterization of [Goldwater] as an extremist was a terrible distortion."[23] Journalist Robert Spero, in his 1980 book *The Duping of the American Voter: Dishonesty and Deception in Presidential Television Advertising*, cited Johnson's 1964 advertising as a particularly egregious example of dishonest voter manipulation. "The extinction of humankind as we know it through the deliberate or accidental misuse of nuclear weapons (and nuclear energy) is not a subject that can be discussed responsibly in a commercial," Spero declared. "The subject is so intense, so complicated, so enormous in its implications and repercussions, and so misunderstood, when measured against the everyday lives of most people, that the attempt to encapsule it within an everyday commercial format was as irresponsible a gesture toward the uninformed public as it was damaging to Goldwater's candidacy."[24]

Even some of Johnson's advisors, particularly Bill Moyers and Lloyd Wright, later worried about the impact their advertising campaign had on political discourse. Some of them may have had those concerns immediately after the election. In 1971, Broder recounted a postcampaign conversation with a group of unnamed Johnson's staff members. "They described, with what I can only call lip-smacking glee," Broder wrote, "the way in which they had foisted on the American public a picture of Barry Goldwater as the nuclear-mad bomber who was going to saw off the eastern seaboard of the United States and end everyone's social security benefits." Broder recalled that near the end of "an almost sensual description of how they had manipulated and maneuvered all this, one of them apparently thought that an ethical comment was called for. 'The only thing that worries me, Dave,' he said, 'is that some year an outfit as good as ours might go to work for the *wrong* candidate.'"[25]

As this book demonstrates, however, Johnson's campaign did not manipulate or mischaracterize the facts about Goldwater and his record. It attributed no words to Goldwater that he had not spoken. Indeed, in the most controversial Johnson spot—Daisy Girl—Goldwater's name and image were absent. The fact is that Goldwater's record over many years was replete with references to the use of nuclear weapons. In one case (talking about lobbing a bomb into the men's room of the Kremlin) he was clearly joking and not seriously proposing an attack on Russia. That, however, begs the question: Why, given the gravity of the times, would a serious candidate for president think it funny to joke about using nuclear weapons? On another occasion, discussing giving NATO commanders control over the use of nuclear weapons in the field, Goldwater protested that his words were misinterpreted; he had meant giving only the supreme NATO military commander such authority. Yet, if Goldwater fully understood the growing perception of him as reckless and extreme, it is inconceivable that he would not have appreciated why such comments might be cause for alarm and, thus, moderated his subsequent rhetoric about war and nuclear weapons. He did not.

The Kremlin joke and the NATO remarks give Goldwater's defenders the best opportunity for arguing that his campaign was, at worst, slandered and, at best, caricatured. The problem is that the occasions were not isolated incidents. Viewed under the most favorable light, questions still remain about Goldwater's judgment. As a U.S. senator, he should have known that words spoken by a potential president, about nuclear weapons, would be treated with deadly seriousness by the press and the public. It appears that either he was unaware of his own public image, oblivious to the consequences of his language as a presidential candidate, or he did know and yet was willing to stubbornly double down on the perception just to make the point that he would not be bullied into trimming his sails to win an election. None of those options suggests that he was the kind of restrained, contemplative sort to whom Americans would entrust control of nuclear weaponry.

Had these been the only reckless statements about nuclear weapons, then the case advanced by Goldwater and his allies would be much stronger. The problem with the criticism of the Daisy Girl and other DDB spots is that critics must find a way to dismiss or rationalize Goldwater's years of reckless and uninformed statements about war and nuclear weapons. One option is to suggest that Goldwater did not mean what he said on numerous occasions—in which case he was not the honest, straightforward man many historians and journalists have portrayed him to be. The other, more reasonable option is to take him at his word over many years and in numerous speeches, interviews, and several books. The overwhelming evidence indicates that he did not regard war with the Soviet Union as a potential calamity to avoid but rather an opportunity to embrace. And he did not regard nuclear weapons as fearsome, apocalyptic weapons to be used only as a last resort, and then only in self-defense, but rather as just another tool in the country's military arsenal.

To read and examine Goldwater's words over many years—and to take him at his word—one must conclude that he was far more likely to consider using nuclear weapons than Lyndon Johnson (although, ironically, Johnson would soon prove himself, in Vietnam, to be no more a peacemaker than Goldwater). That, of course, was not just Johnson's view. It was a view that millions of Americans had formed about Goldwater—long before the Daisy Girl spot was shown on national television. Johnson's campaign, as political scientist John G. Geer has argued, was addressing arguably "the most important issue of the time: nuclear war. It was presenting that theme against the backdrop of Goldwater's own statements about the possible use of nuclear weapons. So why should it be so unreasonable to raise an issue that was most threatening to the lives of the American people and alert voters to what candidates have said about such an important matter."[26] As Scott Jacobs observed in his analysis of the spot after reviewing Goldwater's rhetoric, "Given this situation, I think it is only fair to concede that one could reasonably conclude that running a campaign spot like the Daisy ad was not just permissible, but dialectically obligatory."[27]

■ ■ ■

In the years and decades after the 1964 presidential election, Daisy Girl would live on in numerous campaigns. (One place where it would not live on was at DDB, whose website touting the firm's historical significance in the advertising industry contains no mention of the spot or the firm's role in the Johnson campaign.) Candidates continue to copy the spot but never with the same degree of success achieved by Johnson in 1964. Candidates and independent groups aired versions of the spot in 1996, 2000, 2003, and 2010, each with limited impact after a brief spate of publicity. Perhaps because the spot was so original and so stunning in its creativity, the ability of the petal-plucking girl and the mushroom cloud to strike fear in the hearts of voters expended quickly. Furthermore, while the likelihood of a nuclear war between the Soviet Union and the United States was a real concern throughout the remainder of the 1960s and through the early 1980s, Americans never again felt so threatened by nuclear war as they did in the early 1960s. The image of a mushroom cloud has apparently lost much of its ability to terrify voters. But the spirit of Daisy Girl—using the emotions already lurking in the hearts of voters and bringing them to the surface—will live on and grow in increasingly sophisticated advertising campaigns. Emotion—especially fear—as a tool of politicians and their advertising consultants is here to stay.

APPENDIX

When not speaking in person or by phone, Lyndon Johnson's advisors communicated by inner-office memoranda. From late 1963 through the November 1964 election, these men engaged in a robust exchange of ideas and proposals, and voiced concerns about various aspects of their advertising strategy. In this appendix are featured memoranda that provide a more nuanced view of how the advertising strategy was created and how it evolved.

July 8, 1964

TO: Lawrence F. O'Brien
FROM: Henry H. Wilson, Jr.

I suggest that it is time someone said to the President what apparently no one has yet said to him—that he could lose this election, and that he could lose it despite having lined up all the press and the television networks, all the top labor leaders, most of the top business leaders, all of the Negro vote, and perhaps even Lodge and Rockefeller.

I suggest that we're facing a situation brand new in American politics and that we're going to have to throw all the old rules out of the window and play it by ear.

The situation is new because the opposition is peddling three potent commodities:
    (a). Race prejudice:
        (1) When this gets going organized labor can move right out from under its leadership en masse. I've seen it happen too often. Witness Polish Milwaukee and Baltimore County.
        (2) People mislead pollsters on this issue.
        (3) I'm beginning to get intimations that the FEP thing is cutting pretty deeply outside of the South.
        (4) Suburbia is trouble.
    (b). Chauvinism. It's hard to fight talk about killing foreign aid and winning total victory with reason. Basic foreign policy has not been an issue in a presidential campaign since 1920. And we didn't come out well then.
    (c). Simple answers to complicated questions—Readers Digest has built up a circulation of thirty million on just this premise.

Otherwise I'd suggest that the following recent developments are matters of concern:
    1. It's obvious that some real professionals have taken over the Goldwater operation, and that though their efforts through next week necessarily must be directed solely toward the nomination, it is reasonable to assume that thereafter their operation of a na-

tional campaign will be just as cute, especially when you add a few
people like Leonard Hall and Ray Bliss.

2. There's something fishy about the discrepancy between the projections of Joe Alsop and of the Scranton type polls on the one
hand and of the Republican delegates on the other hand. I cannot believe that the people behind these delegations are complete
fools. If they believed these projections I suggest:

    a. They would be raising considerably more noise than they
    now are to influence the convention, and

    b. They would have no interest in staying in the good graces
    of such an obviously disastrous loser.

3. I get sixth sense type signals around that the President's position has deteriorated significantly in the last week or two. If this
is correct it is reasonable to assume that this will continue at least
through the big show next week, when we could get cut up pretty
badly.

What to do about all this is another problem again. But here are a few
thoughts:

    1. The most paralyzing immediate problem on our side is over-
    confidence a la Dewey in 1948. And I'm afraid we're encourag-
    ing it. The bandwagon technique has its advantages but you can't
    get people to work and sacrifice when they see 70% and 80% fig-
    ures. Our estimates of our position have got to come down at some
    point and we'll come nearer getting the work started normally if
    we ease into this early than if we wait until too late and then in-
    duce panic.

    A logical point of departure is the Republican convention.

    We can say reasonably that we've known all along that when a
    candidate is selected it would turn into a contest.

    But these stories should be started.

    2. I think we will make a serious mistake if we let Goldwater float
    free until the Democratic convention. I don't think the President
    should attack him but I think other Democrats should be scientif-
    ically dissecting him. And if there is a movement afoot to stock-
    pile and pass out this ammunition systematically I haven't come
    across it.

    3. I don't think the Wallace potential should be ignored.

    I'll guess that time remainss [sic] for him to file in a number of states in which he has not filed. I'm aware that this has to be worked by remote control, but I think it can be worked. Certainly it should be explored.

4. I suggest that the usual national committee operations are not being vigorously nor effectively administered.

Source: LBJ Library, WHCF, EX PL 2, 3/17/64–4/30/64, Box 83.

MEMORANDUM
July 29, 1964

FOR: BILL MOYERS

FROM: Horace Busby

SUBJECT: Acceptance Speech

This is in response to your request for ideas and suggestions for the President's acceptance speech at the Democratic National Convention.

1.   The Audience

The decisive audience will be in the nation's living rooms—not the Convention Hall. A fireside chat manner is much more to be desired than political rally oratory, although hard steel should glint in the glow of the fireside. The forensics should be modern, untinged with old-fashioned style. (I hope alliteration can be minimized.)

2.   The "Debate" With Goldwater

Unavoidable in the context of the two conventions is the treatment by the public of this acceptance speech as the equivalent of a first round debate exchange with Goldwater. Frankly, the potential is present for the comparison of these two speeches to have nearly as much bearing on the campaign and the election as the opening exchanges on the first Kennedy-Nixon debate in 1960. Several points are pertinent—

a. Generally, we <u>overestimate</u> the President's exposure. In nine months, he has looked into the television cameras and spoken directly to the American people (rather than to the press or some other audience) on fewer than a half dozen occasions. The man himself—his meaning and manner—must be successfully conveyed at this moment of the acceptance speech.

b. Goldwater's appeal until now is much more personal than the President's. The Goldwater followers are addicted to him as the personification of their own ideas of the "heroic." Admired as he may be, the President has not in office exploited the development of the same kind of zealous rapport. To the extent possible, his appearance should convey qualities of courage, political bravery, candor, as well as <u>convincing</u> compassion. Among other things, this means the President saying—for deliberate effect of courage, independence, and freshness—some things public and press would not expect him to say before his own Party.

c. While the President should convey strongly the image of experience, safety, stability, the thrust should be toward the promise of something <u>new.</u> We must not leave the appeal of "newness" all to Goldwater, nor let voters assume they have seen all the President has to offer.

3.   The "Extremism" Issue

The usual strategy of not mentioning the opposition Party or the opposition candidate by name should be refined still further for this appearance. I would recommend the very greatest care to avoid any characterization of the opposition which employs either direct or oblique allusion to "extremism," "hate," etc.

My feelings on this point are strong, as a matter of political strategy. Democrats and the Democratic friends in the press may, unsuspectingly, be dignifying "extremism." We have to keep in mind that people never regard their own strongly held news as wrong—rather, as righteous. "Extremism" is not (at this point) a vote-getting word from the President's lips—the same is true for "hate." The Democratic coalition through the years has been composed of groups which are targets and victims of hate—but, what we forget, these same groups are often haters themselves.

As a thrust for the speech—and the campaign to follow—I believe we must talk graphically and effectively of the consequences of hate. There is a strong pocketbook vote to be affected by depicting what the consequences of race, class, or regional strife would do to our economic prosperity. Goldwater would "take good times away." This can be made understandable and can be sold. We aren't making him "dangerous" in the right way, so far. If we are selling "prosperity," Goldwater must be prosperity's enemy—as well as peace's.

4.   The Votes to Reach For

The President's appeal will necessarily be interpreted in terms of the votes for which he is reaching: i.e., liberal, middle, Eastern, Southern, etc. Personally, I believe he should be given language clearly reaching for the American middle with not too much ethnic or minority appeal in this speech.

5.   Characterizing the "Enemy"

He should be able to characterize the "opposition"—i.e., the forces, factors or groups which stand in the way of prosperity, good times and good hopes for the American middle.

This is a matter of classic political strategy. FDR ran against the economic royalists. Truman against Wall Street. Eisenhower against bureaucrats and other dimly outlined Washington and international co-conspirators. Thus far, in the development of the Johnson Presidency, the enemies he fights have been too scantily identified. Selection and identification of tangible enemies is a precise process and should be treated with the greatest care. This is a matter of considerable importance, however. The lack of identification of economic or international enemies is tending today to cast the Negro into the role of the tormentor and obstacle of the American in the middle.

At this time I have no suggestions specifically on this point. But I do hope consideration will be given for the acceptance speech.

6.   The "Politician" Image

The Goldwater candidacy in 1964 follows a fairly classic Republican pattern as a rally for the righteous amateur against the cynical political professional. This element was present in the Willkie candidacy, the Hoover candidacy, the Eisenhower candidacy and is implicit in the Goldwater candidacy.

Democrats who exalt and venerate the political professional fail to appreciate many times the red flag which politics and politicians constitute for the public conditioned to regarding the profession and its practitioners as the source of their many troubles. It is important, therefore, that the President's statement avoid those nuances which seem to confirm the national image of him—or suspicion of him—as a professional politician. Chief among these is the tradition of promises to everybody. Clearly, in this speech as much as in the November 27 speech to Congress, a laundry list should be avoided. The theme of the Kennedy Inaugural about sacrifice, etc., is a highly desirable theme for the acceptance speech both in the remarks addressed to the nation and those addressed to the Party. An affluent nation does not really want to be told all's well and will be better—we must avoid the rose-glasses backlash of incredulity.

7.   Specific Language

I have no specific language at my fingertips now and think language tends to go stale through long rewritings. I'll send some as it occurs.

One urgent plea: if used, let's look to a great society—not The Great Society.

Source: LBJ Library, Office Files of Horace Busby, Box 42.

DOYLE · DANE · BERNBACH · INC · ADVERTISING · NEW YORK

DATE: August 6, 1964

FROM: G. Abraham   COPIES TO: L. Wright
TO CLIENT: B. Moyers   **CONFIDENTIAL**   J. Graham—DDB
                                                          A. Petcavage
                                                          D. Parisi

RE: DEMOCRATIC NATIONAL COMMITTEE
       Media

The following is a brief outline of the media plan that we have recommended to the Democratic National Committee for the 1964 presidential campaign.

The formal overall media recommendation and its addendums, Parts I and II, have been structured with one basic objective in mind. That objective is to elect President Johnson on November 3rd and to do so, using available advertising funds, as effectively and as efficiently as possible.

As you know, we have recommended that the major portion of the advertising expenditure be allocated to the following media:

Network Television

Spot Television

Spot Radio

Since the Democratic convention will not take place until the end of August, it is recommended that advertising start the week of September 6th and run through Election Eve.

Network Television

We are suggesting that network television be the cornerstone for the advertising campaign.

Network television is universal in coverage in that 92% of all homes in the United States own at least one receiver; it is less expensive to buy than print or radio media at comparable coverage levels; it provides maximum opportunity for copy flexibility, timeliness and immediacy; it creates frequency of repeat exposures and continuity of effort.

We recommend evening television primarily because of our need to reach equally men and women voters.

In all, we are recommending a combination of 17 60-second commercials, 21 5-minute evening programs, 20 5-minute daytime, 4 30-minute programs and 1 60-minute program on November 2nd.

The 5-minute program unit is a particularly inexpensive way to achieve continuing national coverage and frequency of exposure. At an average cost of $21,181.00, they are cheaper than the cost of a single 20-second prime time announcement on a spot basis (estimated at $38,827).

The 20 daytime 5-minute programs provide for extra effort against women voters. There is no more economical way to reach these important voters.

It is our estimate that a minimum of 85% of all television homes in the United States will be reached by Democratic Party programs, and that the average home reached will be exposed to our message at least 10 to 12 times in the campaign via network television.

Spot Television

In 28 states which account for 406 electoral votes, all major population areas will receive approximately 30 spots weekly or 400 rating points per week which for all practical purposes will be reaching 100% of television homes with our messages 4 times each week, or, 32 times during the campaign via spot television alone. (For example, in California, which has 40 electoral votes, the spot effort will reach a population equivalent to 39.7 of the 40 votes.)

In Missouri, with 12 electoral votes, major population areas will receive approximately 300 rating points per week which will be reaching 95% of all television homes 3 times a week, or, 24 times during the campaign.

In 9 other states considered to be of secondary importance, which account for 56 electoral votes, the major population areas will receive approximately 15 spots weekly, or, 200 rating points per week and will be reaching 95% of all television homes with our message 2 times a week, or, 16 times during a campaign.

In 8 additional states accounting for 40 electoral votes, all major population areas will receive approximately 100 rating points per week, will be reaching 75% of television homes with our message once a week, or, 8 times during the campaign via spot television.

Spot Radio

We feel that local spot radio can reinforce effectively and economically the television effort. The major reasons for its use [are] to reach light television viewers and to reach that population segment not accessible at all to evening television. Its use is recommended in 46 states to varying degrees with the most important states getting 60 1-minute spots weekly in major markets, or, a total of 480 announcements during the campaign.

It is our suggestion to schedule these 1-minute commercials in the heavy automobile traffic times ("drive" times) between 7:00 and 9:00 AM and 4:00–6:30 PM weekdays and all day Saturday in order to reach an audience of both men and women and in order to capitalize on the automobile radio audience which adds nearly 40% to the in-home audience at these time periods.

Local Tie-Ins

As you can see, the network television, spot television and spot radio campaign provide opportunities for local and regional candidates to tie in with the national effort.

We hope to be able to prepare for the Committee a list of cleared network programs, spot radio and television schedules for each state in enough advance time so that corresponding local purchases can be made.

To make the tie-in plan effective (particularly in connection with the broadcast programs), however, requires immediate effort against clearances since negotiating for adjacent spot times and preparation of material locally must, in turn, be done in advance of air dates.

Therefore, it is very desirable to reach decisions at the earliest possible time on network and spot commitments particularly to initiate full clearance reports.

Summary

Media	Geographic Area	Electoral Votes	Cost
Network TV	U.S.	538	$1,964,195.00
Spot TV	46 States	514	4,291,605.00
Spot Radio	46 States	514	1,417,982.00
		Total	$7,673,782.00

As we have mentioned in previous meetings concerning spot television and radio purchasing, stations will expect payments in advance. It will, therefore, be necessary for us to give them certified checks with our orders. Since spot television and radio are non-cancellable for the first 28-day period and cancellable thereafter at any time on two weeks notice, we will need funds to cover the first four spot weeks before we make commitments. The agency feels that this media plan will get the job done effectively and efficiently if it is implemented according to the timetable that we have discussed. However in the case of spot television and radio, any delay in giving us the authority to start purchasing time will hamper our ability to achieve our goals.

Source: LBJ Library, Office Files of Horace Busby, Box 42.

August 17, 1964

Honorable Bill D. Moyers
Special Assistant to the President
The White House
Washington, D.C.

Dear Bill,

If a decision isn't taken immediately to activate the television advertisement plans, there might be serious consequences for the campaign. This is no time for me to be tactful with you. There is too much at stake.

No one knows better than you why we took on the Presidential campaign. There is only one reason. We are ardent Democrats who are deadly afraid of Goldwater and feel that the world must be handed a Johnson landslide. To play our small part in the achievement of such victory we risked the possible resentment of some of our giant Republican clients (I personally told one it was none of his business when he phoned me about our action) and we had to turn away companies who wanted to give us their accounts on a long term basis. Two of the other agencies you were considering withdrew out of fear of their clients. A third agency blithely withdrew and took the Goldwater account.

I tell you all this only to emphasize that we are dedicated people and that our recommendations have a single motivation, not how much money can Doyle Dane Bernbach make, but what is necessary to do the job well. For anyone in your organization who is not a communications expert to pass on our plan is a great mistake. The decision must be made on the same basis that Secretary McNamara said the Defense budget decision was made: "What arms do we need to be the strongest nations [sic] in the world. Then, and only then, see how economically we can achieve our goal." Our plans were made with expert knowledge of what it takes to saturate the nation with the Democratic message. Ignorance in these matters can lead to waste and even disaster.

It is dangerous to think that because Lyndon Johnson is the President of the United States, he will get enough exposure through news coverage to assure him election in November. I don't have to remind you that an exposure on TV or radio or a quote in the nation's press is not necessarily a call to action.

The recommendation, at the volume originally agreed upon, was set as a maximum effort—an ideal campaign. The thought being to permit you to trim where necessary in the interest of political or financial necessity.

I understand you now feel we should suspend all ordering and production on everything we have recommended except the network time already purchased.

We consider the local spot TV and spot radio as absolutely essential to the goal of commanding the necessary share of mind required to get the votes we need for President Johnson in November.

I refer you to the attached media flow chart. Everything not currently on non cancellable order with the networks is crossed out in red. It is immediately apparent that the remaining schedule is grossly inadequate for the eight week period of the campaign. The stakes are just too high to neglect taking maximum advantage of a medium that reaches 92.5% of all homes in the United States. There is no denying the influence television had on the last election; and in 1964 there are 8,550,000 more television sets in use in this country than there were in 1960.

I urgently request that you reconsider and permit us to proceed on the original recommendation at once. If it is necessary to make some adjustment because of financial necessity we will work with you on making a realistic adjustment. The need for immediate action can't be expressed too strongly. Assuming agreement on a spot TV and spot radio schedule next week, and assuming the necessary money being released for use at the same time, the earliest nationwide air date we can make would be the third week of September. This is inflexible. The simple logistics of purchasing, production and shipping preclude any miracles in shortening the time needed.

We agreed that a very necessary part of the campaign is that part devoted to exposing to the voting public the absurd, contradictory and dangerous nature of the opposition candidate. It was agreed that this part of the campaign should be undertaken immediately following our Convention. It is already apparent Barry Goldwater is making every effort to adjust his extreme position to one more acceptable. Knowing the short memory span of the average person, it is entirely possible he might succeed in creating a new character for himself if we are unable to remind people of the truth about this man.

If a decision is delayed until after the Convention, it is obvious that the action resulting from that decision might be "too little and too late."

I urge your immediate attention to this important matter.

Sincerely,

William Bernbach

Source: LBJ Library, Office Files of Horace Busby, Box 42.

THE WHITE HOUSE
WASHINGTON

September 7, 1964

FOR THE PRESIDENT:

Here are suggestions on what the [*sic*] course the campaign should take. It is based on the polls and what they reveal—on conversations with newsmen and state political leaders—and on what has been written in the various newspapers. It assumes some validity in all the above three sources.

I.   FACT: Our main strength lies not so much in the FOR Johnson but in the AGAINST Goldwater.

> Therefore: We ought to treat Goldwater not as an equal, who has credentials to be President, but as a <u>radical,</u> a preposterous candidate who would ruin this country and our future.

> Method: Humor, barbs, jokes, ridicule. If we lambast him in rebuttal, if we answer his charges seriously, if we accept him as a legitimate candidate, we will be elevating him.
>
> Practically all our answers ought to be mantled in ridicule. We ought to get some gag writers to destroy Goldwater-Miller with barbed replies, garmented in humor. We must make him ridiculous and a little scary: trigger-happy, a bomb thrower, a radical, absurd to be President, wonderful local chamber of commerce President but not the Nation's leader, will sell TVA, cancel Social Security, abolish the government, stir trouble in NATO, be the herald of World War III.
>
> We must depict Miller as some April Fool's gag—cannot possibly consider him Vice President material. Show absentee record, lack of confidence in him by his own constituents.

We must treat as first objective: Maintaining in the public mind the firm fear that Goldwater as President would be a vast national joke if it weren't so dangerous to imagine. If we treat him seriously, we will surely lose support.

II. FACT: It is becoming certain that as the campaign goes forward the main thrust of Goldwater-Miller will be to demean the President—the smell of scandal, Bobby Baker, Estes, McCloskey, immorality, thievery, Johnson family fortune, TV station, etc.

Therefore: We should attack on two levels. First, to establish the origin of the Johnson family fortune—based on one thing and one thing only: the appreciation of the worth of a TV station. Once this has been firmly rooted, it is difficult to make credible some supposed wrong-doing.

And second, to hit Goldwater-Miller HARD through other voices of their own immorality of the Republican party.

Method: First, to show the appreciation of the general run of TV stations. Show specific appreciation of a dozen or so TV stations in other cities, how they have grown in value.

Attack Goldwater-Miller for refusal to show sources of income. Intimate Miller has connections with pin-ball operators. Cite Goldwater's mother on payroll. (He wants old people to take care of themselves without government help, yet he uses fraudulent write-off to support his own mother.)

Strike hard at John Byrnes on Baker case and Representative Anderson on Billie Sol Estes. Goldwater's connections with gamblers.

Our objective here: To establish Goldwater-Miller as candidates of contradiction—and almost laughable as candidates for the two top offices.

We need to set forth the opposites [*sic*] of Goldwater's statements. He needs to be shown up as totally incredible.

SO:
1. Treat the ticket as a joke. Theme: This would be funny if it weren't so serious. Use gags, barbs of humor.

2. Don't rebut seriously. Don't bring G-M up to the J-H level.

3. Only strike seriously when they take up the nuclear issue again.

4. Attack Republicans before being attacked on specific immorality within the Republicans.

5. Lay groundwork for source of Johnson family fortune: appreciation of the TV station value.

6. Keep <u>fear</u> of Goldwater as unstable, impulsive, reckless in public's mind. This is our strongest asset. Don't let up on the possibility of Goldwater dismantling Federal government—specific hits on Social Security, TVA, farm subsidies.

7. Never let up on "contradictions." Show and show again how he is on all sides of question. This is the best way to prove instability, uncertainty.

8. Finally, President stays above the battle. He is President and acts like one.

Jack Valenti

Source: LBJ Library, WHCF, EX PL 2, 9/6/64–9/14/64, Box 84.

THE WHITE HOUSE
WASHINGTON

September 13, 1964

Mr. President:

While most of our radio-television campaign is to project you and your record, we decided—as you may recall—to run a few of the earlier spots just
to "touch up" Goldwater a bit and remind people that he is not as moderate
as his recent speeches want them to believe he his. The idea was not to let
him get away with building a moderate image and to put him on the defensive before the campaign is very old.

I think we succeeded in our first spot—the one on the control of nuclear
weapons.

It caused his people to start defending him right away. Yesterday Burch said:
"This ad implies that Senator Goldwater is a reckless man and Lyndon Johnson a careful man." Well, that's exactly what we wanted to imply. And we
also hoped someone around Goldwater would say it, not us. They did. Yesterday was spent in trying to show that Goldwater isn't reckless.

Furthermore, while we paid for the ad only on NBC last Monday night, ABC
and CBS both ran it on their news shows Friday. So we got it shown on all
three networks for the price of one.

This particular ad was designed to run only one time. We have a few more
Goldwater ads, more as hard-hitting as that one was, and then we go pro-
Johnson, pro-Peace, Prosperity, Preparedness spots.

Bill Moyers

Source: LBJ Library, Office Files of Bill Moyers, Box 39.

September 14, 1964

MEMORANDUM FOR: Bill Moyers
                   Mike Feldman
                   Fred Dutton

1. If we are not careful, G-M are going to usurp the ridicule area from us.

Have we got working with us daily a gag-writer, a comic man, a whip-cracker line-man (such as Abe Burrows, etc.)?

If we are not careful, the Goldwater image will get all smoothed up to our detriment. Right now, the biggest asset we have is Goldwater's alleged instability in re[:] atom and hydrogen bombs. We MUST NOT let this slip away.

"A-Bomb Barry"—"wagons in a circle" etc. need to be in every speech-maker's kit—and we need to whack at him EVERY day with gags and humor that deny him any right to be called sane or stable.

Cartoons—the Herblock variety (including that ageless classic WHY DON'T YOU SHOW INITIATIVE AND INHERIT YOURSELF A DEPARTMENT STORE) ought to be reprinted by the thousands and distributed.

2. MEET THE PRESS yesterday was a good case in point of keeping the enemy on the defensive. Miller was kept so busy denying charges he had no opportunity to attack. Have we got our people on Miller and Goldwater backgrounds—so that we can supply newsmen with questions to ask and facts to back up their questions? This is vital.

3. Why haven't we hit the pages with a denouncing of Miller and his immigration speech? If we don't do it within the next two days, it will be old hat. We simply can't let him off the hook on this. Why can't ethnic leaders wire him to resign as nominee—or wire Goldwater to take him off the ticket—or ask Goldwater if he subscribes to Miller's beliefs, and if he doesn't demand he have Miller apologize. We can't let this GOLDEN opportunity fade away.

Jack Valenti

Source: LBJ Library, WHCF, EX PL 2, 9/6/64–9/14/64, Box 84.

MEMORANDUM FOR LLOYD WRIGHT

FROM: Bill Moyers

Some suggestions for spots . . . .

Barry Goldwater wants to be President. Well, if Senator Goldwater were successful in that ambition

— He <u>could</u> be in a position to withdraw the United States from the United Nations—one of mankind's best hopes for peace and freedom since its founding.

Only two years ago he said that's what we ought to do.

— He could have his finger—or that of some field commander—on the nuclear trigger.

That's what he wants to do.

— He could be in a position to destroy the nuclear test-ban treaty which has halted the pollution of the atmosphere.

That's what his policies would do.

— He could be in a position to make the social security program voluntary. He has said that's what he wants to do—although responsible men know that would destroy social security.

He <u>could</u> do these things—

But only if we let him.

Vote for President Johnson on November 3. The stakes are too high to stay home.

Senator Barry Goldwater has recently been trying to sound like a man of peace.

But in an interview on May 8, 1961, Senator Goldwater said he doesn't see how a real nuclear war can be avoided. He said it could come in perhaps five, or ten years from now.

And in the Los Angeles Times on November 15, 1961, Senator Goldwater said he would drop a low-yield atomic bomb in North Vietnam.

What's more, in Hartford, Connecticut, Senator Goldwater—only last year—said that the President of the United States should permit military commanders in Europe to use tactical nuclear weapons on their own initiative.

If Barry Goldwater really wants peace, he is going after it in a peculiar way.

No matter what he says now, to win votes, his record speaks for itself—and for him.

Vote for President Johnson on November 3. The stakes are too high for you to stay home.

Source: LBJ Library, WHCF, EX PL 2, 9/6/64–9/14/64, Box 84.

September 18, 1964

MEMORANDUM FOR   BILL
FROM   HAYES

Reflections of New York Trip

1. I'm worried about [the] count-down ad. We cannot let people forget
    BMG's nuclear irresponsibility but I'm wary about throwing more
    bombs around. We already have people worried about Barry the
    Bomber. Scare ads could have what Scammon called an "overkill" effect.
    Perhaps serious responsible reminders would be better.

2. In addition to the problems you raised about "confessions" it seems to
    me that the guy looks and acts phony, stilted and very contrived.

3. In addition to the "Barry No" ad, we could combine both the positive
    LBJ and the anti-BMG themes in a single "yes-no" ad which would also
    help us around sticky problems like the word "voluntary," etc. Some-
    thing like the following:

    We will not destroy Social Security[.]

    We will fight for health insurance for the elderly[.]

    We will not sell the TVA.

    We will work for greater development of our natural resources.

    We will not give control of nuclear weapons to field commanders.

    We will maintain responsibility in the White House where it belongs,
    etc.

4. On the way back, John Hayes expressed considerable concern about the
    production and distribution schedules.

Source: LBJ Library, Office Files of Bill Moyers, Box 39.

DEMOCRATIC NATIONAL COMMITTEE

1730 K STREET, N.W.

WASHINGTON, D.C.   20006

September 21, 1964

MEMORANDUM TO: Bill Moyers
The White House

FROM: Fred Dutton

SUBJECT: Possible Personal Attacks on the President

In seeking to anticipate the course of the campaign during the final six weeks, and especially the likely main thrust of the opposition, the so-called "integrity issue" seems to be the last main battleground on which Goldwater will likely try to make a stand.

He has aggressively tried out all of his other major issues, and they have generally backfired. He has fenced with personal attacks on the President but each time seemed to be trying to lay a foundation rather than follow through with a massive assault. In the meantime, at the grass roots, reportedly over 7 million copies of Haley's slander and similar book-sized tracts have been distributed, plus millions of scurrilous tabloids and other material. In effect, an attempted softening up has been going on—but the all-out assault by Goldwater himself has not yet occurred. He really has no alternative but to go with it hard sometime in the next several weeks.

We will win overwhelmingly regardless of what he does. But such an attack can blemish long-term public attitudes toward the President unless it is anticipated and shown up from the outset. In anticipation of such an attack the following action on our part should be considered:

1. The President's schedule and personal calls should include an increased number of the kind of people who are not political but subconsciously considered by most of the public a part of the moral leadership of the country—individuals like Billy Graham, Cardinal Spellman, Bishop

Pike of San Francisco, Reverend Blake, Carl Sandburg, Justice Frankfurter, President Robert Goheen of Princeton. These are reassuring public symbols to publicly <u>identify</u> with in a non-political relationship—before front page personal attacks are mounted.

2. <u>Fuller passages of moral leadership should be considered for at least the closing section of Presidential speeches.</u> I realize there is already much text along those lines. But more emphatic use of it would be useful without appearing to be obvious.

3. <u>More Presidential speeches on human needs, supplementing the emphasis on peace, national security, etc.,</u> will help more people to feel a closer personal bond with the President. The peace issue is clearly the overriding one of this election. More emphasis on human problems and leadership for young people would help strengthen the President's role as educator and moral leader for the nation.

4. <u>The campaign itself has got to keep pressing to put Goldwater on the defensive</u>—on nuclear bombs, his contradictions, and personality. Political attack is still the best defense! Too much of public opinion still seems to say that Goldwater may be badly informed, but he is at least a man of conviction. That conclusion is nonsense; but we have not yet effectively demonstrated to the satisfaction of the general public that in terms of changing his position on issues, he is not really a man of conviction, or integrity. Humphrey needs to pound away at that; and we need two tough newsworthy curmudgeons who weigh into this attack practically everyday. I suggest as possibilities Franklin Roosevelt, possibly Udall as an Arizonan, and John McCormack and President Truman could also undoubtedly be urged to land a couple of real haymakers.

5. <u>When finally the personal attack comes, if it does, we must meet it promptly and sharply</u> with several highly respected spokesmen who will bring the accuser to account in disbelief. They should not be political leaders but prestige people somewhat outside of politics, as possibly Robert Lovitt, John McCloy, Bishop Pike, or General Omar Bradley. We probably should have ready in advance channels to activate people like that when and if needed.

Source: LBJ Library, Office Files of Bill Moyers, Box 39.

THE WHITE HOUSE
WASHINGTON

September 22, 1964

MEMORANDUM FOR
   Bill Moyers

IDEAS

Traveling, I get the impression Goldwater did not get off the ground at the start—that he scattered his shots too widely, hit too many issues, and thus diffused his impact; that when he hit little issues, he seemed far beneath the presidential level, particularly since the headlines posed such awesome perils and problems; and that on the big issues, he scared people and is on the defensive on the nuclear issue (which is THE issue, I think.)

His more recent attack on the TVA at Knoxville and on the poverty program in Appalachia seem[s] calculated to enhance his standing as a Man of Courage and Principle, to counter the accusation that he changes his mind. This, plus his challenge to debate, seems calculated to stake out an underdog position. Since he started with support that was deep and fervent but narrow, his best hope of broadening his support—which he must do—would seem to lie in setting in motion a strong underdog tie. So far it doesn't seem to be running—but it might.

The President, starting with very broad but rather shallow support, has held that support by his "non-political" above-the-battle stance (while lower officials and candidates keep Goldwater busy). His non-partisan stance, however, does not seem to have countered the most common criticism of him: That he is a "politician." As election time nears, it may even backfire—people may think his "non-political" trips are sly efforts to deceive them. Apart from this, to win, his non-political position requires a quiet but powerful local organization effort; and although it is early, such organization effort seems lagging. His own non-political position encourages apathy and over confidence in local organizations (and factionalism—quarreling over the sports of a victory taken for granted). Moreover, this non-political position does not deepen the President's support—if he is not fighting, why should they. His broad support could be threatened if Goldwater started broadening his own support on an underdog tide—or if the people got the idea the President was "taking them for granted."

In sum, the big "landslide" trend to the President seems to be more anti-Goldwater trend than a pro-LBJ trend.

The President may want to consider these ideas:

(1) About October 1, he may want to go on national TV from his office for a non-political report to the people on the state for peace. Peace is our best issue. So far it has been working against Goldwater. If the President could find an appropriate time, he might make it work for him. People are uneasy, and some may feel the President owes them a report. If he makes one, it should be candid.

(2) Continue to refuse to answer Goldwater himself in the hope he will, in desperation, start swinging wildly (e.g., outright anti-Negro, outright pro-war in Viet Nam or Cuba); then, after the World Series the traditional time when such organizations as that in Chicago go to work, pick up on his wild swings, attack him head-on, show that he threatens not only the peace but jobs and social security and everything else, and keep hitting him till the election.

Two specifics for possible actions soon:

(1) Attack the issue of violence in the cities obliquely by tackling the school dropout problem substantively. E.g., at John[s] Hopkins University he might say he is more concerned about those absent from the audience than those present—the dropouts—and he might, (after, of course, careful private groundwork) announce appointment of a commission on dropouts to be headed by Milton Eisenhower (or Conant or someone else). He might also get mileage out of a concomitant White House meeting of Mayors, educators, and sociologists on dropouts, also bringing in Sarge Shriver, and others involved in the Peace Corps and Poverty Program. Hopefully, a five-point program for combating dropout-itis and salvaging dropouts would emerge in a couple of weeks (if desired).

(2) Viet Nam: Absent any improvement there, would it be worth considering for the President to either (a) exchange messages with the Pope and the Chief Buddhist (I gather Buddhism has no "Pope" but has, rather, local

autonomy, which is troublesome to stop killings on humanitarian grounds; or (b) meet with DeGaulle (and possibly Lord Home) while deGaulle is in our Hemisphere.

John Bartlow Martin

Source: LBJ Library, Office Files of Bill Moyers, Box 6.

DEMOCRATIC NATIONAL COMMITTEE
1730 K STREET, N.W.
WASHINGTON, D.C. 20006

September 26, 1964

MEMORANDUM TO BILL MOYERS
        The White House

SUBJECT: Criteria for Campaign Speeches and Related Projects in
           October
FROM: Fred Dutton

Here are some criteria that I believe should be considered in drawing up the President's speeches and special projects for the October campaign period:

1.   His Presidential role is obviously our strongest campaign asset—it should be kept clearly in public focus in the weeks ahead. This means that while the President has to get around the country and show vigor and closeness to the people, he should also get back into the White House frequently and have showcase opportunities arranged there. In brief, he needs to be President as much as possible even during October and appear as a candidate only to a moderate extent. Inevitable campaign pressures to raise money all over the country and engage in endless brainstorming will have to be resisted. His tentative schedule, in fact, is already heavily booked; and endless requests for additional appearances lie ahead. In terms of present day communications, which is the real problem at hand, we are in the age of mass media, especially television—not the whistlestops and political rituals dear to most of our hearts but really part of a period that went out with Truman as far as the overwhelming majority of people are concerned.

2.   The President is not at his most effective on television when speaking in outdoor settings, where he is often either too quiet or too strident—I am not even sure that he is most persuasive in direct television talks, where his southern accent comes through a little too directly for national television audiences used to northern or nonregional types. I consequently urge

that the inevitable flood of speeches be intermingled as much as possible with action or doing situations. That should also help reinforce the emphasis on his ongoing Presidential role rather than candidate position.

To the extent television appearances are undertaken (after the first one of him opening his campaign), I suggest that consideration be given to using the format of small conversation groups with him, as Rusk, Stevenson and McNamara on foreign policy questions; Dillon and Wirtz (or possibly even Meany or Henry Ford II) on the economy; several prestige interviewers like Lippmann, Reston and Ralph McGill, or three nominees of the networks; and finally Hubert Humphrey.

3. Although Goldwater will almost certainly be beaten overwhelmingly, our opposition will likely use October to try to blemish the President's long-term public standing as much as possible—the wheeler-dealer charge will almost surely be the main underlying theme to which they will keep returning. In addition to that, the press already gives considerable indication that while it is solidly against Goldwater, it will interpret the election not as a Johnson victory, or pro Democratic or for any particular program mandate but only a disconsolate rejection. The quality of the campaign we offer, and the solid substance of the proposals the President makes, will be the only really effective way to overcome those inevitable criticisms. This means the speeches should project more farseeing goals and suggest more specific proposals than has really been done thus far.

4. A related consideration for the President personally is that (particularly with his almost certainly winning big) we need to look at how he uses this opportunity with the country to help build his public leadership for the next several years and how history will judge what he did and said in his own first national campaign: what goals he raised, what influence he exerted and what new energies he stirred in the country. A campaign, of course, is a political, not substantive exercise. But the President is now so far ahead that he can and should so use this opportunity to go to the country to serve several purposes.

This consideration, like the preceding one, militates for him to shape at least a broad basic mandate more clearly than has been done to date. We must so project our campaign that the press cannot interpret the election mostly as a rejection of Goldwater and extremism (as profoundly constructive as that will be)—but as a mandate to reduce world tensions and make domestic headway. We also need to be careful that our emphasis on unity does not lead any of the several major segments making up our impressive coalition to plausibly claim later that they were mislead [sic] or should have a veto on future programs. This is particularly true in relation to some of the very conservative press and business support that we have (and certainly want).

In summary, the speeches should (a) keep reemphasizing the major issues (peace, prosperity, extremism, the Democrats will do more for America); (b) appeal to the major groups in the electorate; and (c) do the major political tasks at hand (hold the broad base, keep Goldwater on the defensive, build the momentum of the campaign and get out the vote). But they should also (1) shape a usable mandate for afterwards; (2) reemphasize the quality or prestige and personal warmth of the President; (3) accomplish useful public education on the changing nature of our society; and (4) assure that the President's campaign efforts stand up historically not only in achieving a massive numerical sweep but in providing an important substantive foundation for future action.

In a separate memorandum I will try to make some suggestions on possible specific campaign speech themes and special projects for October. But first we need to shape the ultimate effect we want to establish in the last five weeks and the various problems that must be implicitly handled. Above all, we need to consider the speech drafts not separately but in relation to our television spots and overall effort, the pacing of the campaign, and a schedule that builds interest and momentum for a climatic conclusion.

Source: LBJ Library, Office Files of Bill Moyers, Box 39.

ASSISTANT SECRETARY OF STATE

WASHINGTON

September 29, 1964

<u>PERSONAL</u>

MEMORANDUM FOR: The Honorable
Bill Moyers, Jr.,
Special Assistant to the President

SUBJECT: The Campaign

A close study of the history of American politics might show that extremist political movements reach the surface of political life *after* the fears which motivate them have passed their peak.

I suspect that when we have some more perspective we shall see that cold war frustration reached its peak in this country in the period between the first Sputnik and the Cuban missile crisis and, for sake of convenience, might be symbolized by the apology of C.D. Jackson to Dr. Schwartz in the Hollywood Bowl. Whatever the Birch Society says about membership and despite the claims of Minutemen and Minutewomen, I have the impression that hysteria has been on the decline since the height of the Congo crisis and the hi-jacking of planes for Castro.

If this notion is correct, then Goldwater's candidacy marks the decline and not the rise of American frustration about foreign affairs in general and communism in particular.

And in this event, we can take the Scripps-Howard editorial announcing for President Johnson as an important clue to the most appropriate Democratic behavior for the five-and-a-half weeks of the campaign that remain. Scripps-Howard probably speaks for a sizeable majority of the Midlands and the Mainstream of America when it says—almost reluctantly but with evident relief—that post-war American foreign policy is beginning to pay off and that we better stick with it because it is the sounder and safer thing to do.

The corollary to all this is that people may have had about enough of the "cry-babies" and the "panic-peddlers" and the "scare-mongers."

If so, then we do not have to belabor the danger and the fallacy and the ignorance of the Goldwater psychosis. We can take it for granted that a big majority is with us. We therefore should stress the better days that lie ahead in the world and at home. We should exude confidence in our proven ability to take care of ourselves in the wicked world, to gradually build up a secure world order, and to get on with the Great Society here at home.

We should, in other words, talk more and more about ourselves and the future—and less and less about Goldwaterism and the past.

I think that from now on—instead of letting this campaign degenerate into the predicted skunk-fight—we should largely ignore the "choice" offered by Goldwater and talk it up for the best society yet to see the light of day.

Harlan Cleveland

Source: LBJ Library, Office Files of Bill Moyers, Box 53.

October 1, 1964

MEMORANDUM FOR
Bill Moyers

GENERAL STRATEGY

I feel that Goldwater has probably reached his low point. And we are stalled.

Polls, press, and pols are discouraging the Goldwater people, except the fanatics. They are breeding overconfidence and indifference among Democrats.

It can be argued that this helps Goldwater. He can only go up, and if he does, he might suddenly broaden his original narrow but deep support. We started with broad but shallow support, started too high too soon. It is possible that those whom Goldwater shocked and scared at first will have learned to live with him by November.

On the other hand, his troubles with Romney and Keating and Percy and others, the polls, the President;s [sic] refusal to reply to his attacks may provoke Goldwater into new extremism. Some evidence hints this may be already happening: In the last few days he has cried "soft on communism" and "liar." The pressures on Goldwater must be enormous. He complained last week about his heavy schedule; This week he is making a back-breaking whistlestop tour in the Midwest. If he blows up, he is finished.

I think the President should stay high, ignoring him, driving him crazy, and hoping, by silence, to provoke him into a blowup.

At the same time, the President can't stand still but must deepen his own support. He has given the people something to vote against—Goldwater. Perhaps now he should give them something to vote for.

For, unfortunately, as of now, the President's votes appear to be anti-Goldwater, not pro-Johnson. The campaign has aroused little interest or enthusiasm, considerable disappointment, and some disgust. It is a hard, harsh, barren campaign. It lacks warmth and excitement. And there is too much interest in non-presidential races (Kennedy in New York, Percy in Illinois, etc.) This could cut into the President's vote. And to break the back of know-nothingism and racism and extremism, and to govern well, the President needs to win big.

Many people think this a "strange" campaign, as though the nation were going through a meaningless dumb show. They don't like it.

The President must not seem, by staying lofty, to be taking the people for granted; nothing could be more dangerous. They want to see him.

I think the President should stay high and non-partisan.

But I think the time has come to fire the second-stage rocket. I suggest this involves three things:

(1) A television talk to the people by the President from his office, perhaps on peace, but rather, I think, on the campaign itself. The President needs a direct link to the people in this campaign. He might tell them he has hoped the campaign would illuminate issues and clarify choices, that he has been disappointed, that henceforward he will take the issues to the people insofar as his official duties will permit, that he had hoped the campaign would not prove divisive and corrosive in this dangerous time and that he is still determined to prevent it from becoming so.

(2) In campaigning—and the people <u>do</u> want to see him—the President might deliver speeches that are, or seem to be, programmatic. Dangers inhere in this: Offering program inevitably draws fire; for an incumbent President to offer one is tantamount to making up a budget ad hoc; and Goldwater will outpromise him.

The alternative is an attack on Goldwater. But this, I think, is what bothers people about the campaign already—too much name-calling, no substance. And it would play into Goldwater's hands, cut the President down to Goldwater's size. The President could make, if not actually programmatic speeches, at least constructive substantive ones. He needs to <u>say something</u> during the next three weeks. About October 25 he may want to shift over to the attack, depending on the situation then, and keep slugging to the end. But now, I think, he should stake out positions on great issues appropriate to a statesman: Defense; foreign policy; economic growth for continued prosperity; the condition of our cities; the roads to peace. These speeches need not be dull. They need not be a-political. They can be interesting, knowledgeable, sensible, responsible—and they should ignore Goldwater. It is difficult to give such substantive speeches to big crowds on the road. Perhaps the President could deliver them on national television, from his office, and speak briefly on the same themes while on the road. Once or twice he might fly to a city, deliver a major substantive speech from a television studio, and merely shake hands and deliver a few remarks at one or two places in the city. (e.g., Citizens for Johnson-Humphrey headquarters). He does not need to go to the people in person.

(3) We should unleash a lot of local hoopla not involving the President (citizens for Johnson-Humphrey, independents for Johnson-Humphrey, intellectuals for Johnson-Humphrey, committees of all kinds), and a good deal of what they do should be exciting and fun. This is a drab gray campaign.

I suggest the President take Mrs. Johnson with him wherever possible, especially into the Midwest. (I found quite a few Midwestern suburban housewives who spoke very warmly of her.)

In sum:

To counter know-nothingism, the President should seem very knowledgeable; to counter disappointment in the empty campaign, go programmatic or at least substantive; to counter disappointment at the "cold" campaign, appear in company with Mrs. Johnson; to point up Goldwater's scary trigger-happiness, seem calm and confident and safe; to point up Goldwater's foolish scattergun attack, stay on three themes—peace, prosperity, and unity.

Finally, I think the President himself, and perhaps everyone else, should drop the nuclear issue now. It is cemented in; Nothing Goldwater can do will shake it. If the President keeps hitting it, it may backfire, because it's complicated. Or people may just learn to live with it, develop an immunity. In the last week, I suggest the President raise the issue again and hammer it home in the end. It is, I think our one best issue, and must be used with care. (Incidentally, I tried this idea out on Dick Daley; he agrees completely.)

John Bartlow Martin

Source: LBJ Library, Office Files of Bill Moyers, Box 25.

DEMOCRATIC NATIONAL COMMITTEE

1730 K STREET, N.W.

WASHINGTON D.C.   20006

KENNETH O'DONNELL
EXECUTIVE DIRECTOR

TELEPHONE
FEDERAL 3-8750

October 20, 1964

MEMORANDUM TO: The President

FROM: Kenneth O'Donnell

We have surveyed the recent developments in the last week, and their effect upon your candidacy, in as much depth as possible in such a brief period of time. It is practically the unanimous opinion that, on balance, the situation in the Soviet Union has outweighed the events here on the Domestic front and that they have in reality either cancelled each other out, or reflected a small increase in favor of the continuation of the stewardship of the Democratic Party.

Frankly, my personal conversations with political people around the country do reflect a genuine uneasiness as to the long-range effect of our problem and as to any future exploitation of the Republican Party on this issue. There has been an almost total Republican concentration now on the issue of scandal and a mess in Washington caused, in the main, by their utter failure to make any impact upon the voters on any of the other issues of the campaign, in either domestic or international spheres.

Your broadcast on Sunday was well received. I feel the main effort of our campaign for the next two weeks should be to seize the initiative from the Republicans on as high a level as possible, and we should endeavor to make a newsworthy statement every day, on a high level, to continue to present the contrast between the gutter campaign they will employ in the next two weeks.

The Committee unanimously urges that position papers and suggestions of new programs for 1965 should be forthcoming as rapidly as possible. This was strongly urged upon Mr. Feldman, Mr. Dutton, and I'm hopeful was transmitted to Billy Moyers. A strong, issue-oriented, high-level program, discussing the future programs and activities of President Johnson in 1965 is needed now, and can serve as the most effective answer to Republican attacks.

Television

It is our option, and it is shared by all our people in the field, that our television has been most ineffective. We have used the same spots over and over until they have outlived their usefulness. They are a tremendous drain on the finances of the National Committee and we strongly urge that they be discontinued and that the television immediately transfer its thrust to presenting programs of the Administration's past, and also the new legislation and new goals that Lyndon B. Johnson will implement in 1965. It would be much more effective if the President himself presented these spots, outlining a new program which would then become a news story the following day, rather than repetitious spots that have outworn their welcome.

Any new spots should be directed at getting out the vote, at Democrats, and the Agency should keep in mind that it is competing in every state in the Union with local candidates who are also employing television to its fullest extent.

In sum, our problems are two-fold:

To blanket out the Republican smears with progressive, new Democratic proposals that the newspapers will be delighted to print, and far preferably, to television taking that money and investigating it in a vigorous, well-financed, get-out-the-vote program which will get every Democrat to the polls on November 3.

Source: LBJ Library, WHCF, EX PL 2, 10/8/64, Box 85.

NOTES

1. THE ATOM THEME

1. Lyndon Johnson and George Reedy telephone conversation, Aug. 20, 1964, LBJ-wh6408_29_5047_reedy, at www.whitehousetapes.net, hosted by the Miller Center for Public Affairs at University of Virginia.

2. "Secretary Dulles' Strategy of Massive Retaliation," Jan. 12, 1954, *Documents of American History,* vol. 2, 7th ed., ed. Henry Steele Commager (New York: Meredith, 1963), 609–10.

3. Theodore C. Sorenson, *Kennedy* (New York: Harper and Row, 1965), 512.

4. Maxwell D. Taylor, *The Uncertain Trumpet* (New York: Harper, 1950), 5.

5. "The Berlin Crisis," July 25, 1961, *Documents of American History,* vol. 2, 7th ed., ed. Henry Steele Commager (New York: Meredith, 1963), 706–8.

6. Allan M. Winkler, *Life under a Cloud: American Anxiety about the Atom* (New York: Oxford, 1993), 171.

7. "The Berlin Crisis," 706–8.

8. Winkler, *Life under a Cloud,* 122.

9. John T. Woolley and Gerhard Peters, The American Presidency Project, hosted by the University of California, available at www.presidency.ucsb.edu/ws/?pid=8151.

10. Paul Boyer, "From Activism to Apathy: The American People and Nuclear Weapons, 1963–1980," *Journal of American History* 70, no. 4 (March 1984): 823; "The Milk All of Us Drink and Fallout," *Consumer Reports,* March 1959, 102-11.

11. Henry Kissinger, *Diplomacy* (New York: Touchstone, 1994), 571.

12. "The Berlin Crisis," 706–8.

13. Robert Dallek, *An Unfinished Life: John F. Kennedy, 1917–1963* (Boston: Little, Brown, 2003), 421.

14. Ibid., 422.

15. Arthur M. Schlesinger, *A Thousand Days: John F. Kennedy in the White House* (Boston: Houghton Mifflin, 1965), 391.

16. "The Berlin Crisis," 706–8.

17. Dallek, *An Unfinished Life,* 431.

18. "Atmosphere Test," *New York Times,* Sept. 2, 1961; "Test Announcement and Reply," *New York Times,* Sept. 3, 1961; Dallek, *An Unfinished Life,* 429.

19. Dallek, *An Unfinished Life,* 433.

20. Kissinger, *Diplomacy,* 585.

21. Dallek, *An Unfinished Life,* 536.

22. A. A. Fursenko and Timothy J. Naftali, *One Hell of a Gamble: Khrushchev, Castro, and Kennedy, 1958–1964* (New York: Norton, 1997), 182.

23. "Radio and Television Report to the American People on the Soviet Arms Buildup in Cuba," John F. Kennedy Presidential Library, www.jfklibrary.org/jfkl/cmc/j102262.htm.

24. Dallek, *An Unfinished Life,* 558.

25. Arthur M. Schlesinger, *Robert Kennedy and His Times* (Boston: Houghton Mifflin, 1978), 514.

26. Michael Dobbs, *One Minute to Midnight: Kennedy, Khrushchev, and Castro on the Brink of Nuclear War* (New York: Knopf, 2008), 292–93.

27. Dallek, *An Unfinished Life,* 567–71.

28. Richard Reeves, *President Kennedy: Profile of Power* (New York: Touchstone, 1993), 424.

29. Schlesinger, *A Thousand Days,* 841.

30. Dobbs, *One Minute to Midnight,* 349.

31. Gene N. Levine and John Modell, "American Public Opinion and the Fallout-Shelter Issue," *Public Opinion Quarterly* 29, no. 2 (Summer 1965): 270–79.

32. Eugene J. Rosi, "Mass and Attentive Opinion on Nuclear Weapons Tests and Fallout, 1954–1963," *Public Opinion Quarterly* 29, no. 2 (Summer 1965): 280–97.

33. Hazel Gaudet Erskine, "The Polls: Atomic Weapons and Nuclear Energy," *Public Opinion Quarterly* 27, no. 2 (Summer 1963): 155–90.

34. Ralph E. Lapp, "The Strategy of Overkill," *Bulletin of the Atomic Scientists* (April 1963): 4–11.

35. Pat Frank, *How to Survive the H-Bomb . . . and Why* (Philadelphia: J. B. Lippincott, 1962), 9–10.

36. Thomas L. Martin and Donald C. Latham, *Strategy for Survival* (Tucson: University of Arizona Press, 1963), 182–90.

37. Don Oberdorfer, "Survival of the Fewest," *Saturday Evening Post,* Mar. 23, 1963, 17–21.

38. "The Family: Emotions and the Bomb," *Time,* Jan. 4, 1963.

39. D. G. Green, "Letters," *The Nation,* Apr. 18, 1981, 450.

40. Don Oberdorfer, "Survival of the Fewest," *Saturday Evening Post,* Mar. 23, 1963, 17–21.

41. Todd Gitlin, *The Sixties: Years of Hope, Days of Rage* (New York: Bantam, 1987), 22–23.

42. Claude C. Bowman, "The Family and the Nuclear Arms Race," *Social Problems* 11, no. 1, special issue: "The Threat of War: Policy and Public Opinion" (Summer 1963): 29–34.

43. Survey by Gallup Organization, Dec. 13–18, 1962, from the iPOLL Databank, Roper Center for Public Opinion Research, University of Connecticut, www.ropercenter.uconn.edu/data_access/ipoll/ipoll.html; Raymond L. Garthoff, *Reflections on the Cuban Missile Crisis* (Washington: Brookings Institution, 1987), 77–78.

44. "Goldwater Calls Cuba Policy Weak," *New York Times,* Sept. 15, 1962; "Goldwater Demands Stevenson's Ouster," *New York Times,* Nov. 13, 1962; "Goldwater Asks Senate Inquiry Into U.S. Role in Cuba Invasion," *New York Times,* Jan. 24, 1963.

45. "Goldwater Replies to Kennedy," *New York Times,* Apr. 26, 1963.

46. Lee Edwards, *Goldwater: The Man Who Made a Revolution* (Washington: Regnery, 1995), 135–37.

47. "Johnson, in West, Decries Extremism," *New York Times,* Oct. 13, 1964.

48. James T. Patterson, *Grand Expectations: The United States, 1945–1974* (New York: Oxford, 1996), 558.

49. "President Finds G.O.P. 'Smearlash,'" *New York Times,* Oct. 22, 1964.

50. Dallek, *An Unfinished Life,* 690.

51. Reeves, *President Kennedy,* 655.

2. WHY NOT VICTORY?

1. Lee Edwards, *Goldwater: The Man Who Made a Revolution* (Washington: Regnery, 1995), 115.

2. Barry Goldwater, *The Conscience of a Conservative* (New York: Hillman Books, 1960), 25–44, 60–69.

3. Ibid., 39.

4. Ibid., 89-90.

5. Ibid., 91.

6. Ibid., 92-93.

7. Ibid., 112, 122.

8. Ibid., 124-25.

9. Ibid., 88–127, 125.

10. Edwards, *Goldwater,* 128.

11. Rick Perlstein, *Before the Storm: Barry Goldwater and the Unmaking of the American Consensus* (New York: Hill and Wang, 2001), 63.

12. *Congressional Record,* May 18, 1960, 10512–13.

13. "Disarmament: 'Dangerous Promise,'" *Sunday Oregonian,* Dec. 25, 1960.

14. Goldwater, *The Conscience of a Conservative,* 113.

15. *Congressional Record,* May 9, 1962, 8049–52; *Baltimore Sun,* Nov. 13, 1962.

16. "Goldwater Says Threat Is on Left," *New York Times,* June 30, 1963; *Congressional Record,* Sept. 19, 1963, 17557-58.

17. Barry Goldwater, *Why Not Victory? A Fresh Look at American Foreign Policy* (New York: MacFadden, 1962), 25.

18. Ibid., 34.

19. Ibid., 108–9.

20. "A Great Speech," *Life,* Jan. 27, 1961, 24-25.

21. Robert Alan Goldberg, *Barry Goldwater* (New Haven: Yale University Press, 1995), 157.

22. Richard H. Rovere, *The Goldwater Caper* (New York: Harcourt Brace, 1965), 40.

23. "G.O.P. Nominee's Views, in His Own Words, on Major Issues of Campaign," *New York Times,* June 18, 1964; Goldberg, *Barry Goldwater,* 183–84.

24 "Goldwater Favors Sharing Atom Arms with NATO Allies," *New York Times,* Jan. 14, 1964.

25. "Transcript of Unpublished Part of Der Speigel's Interview with Goldwater," *New York Times,* July 11, 1964.

26. "Transcript of Unpublished Part of Der Speigel's Interview with Goldwater," *New York Times*, July 11, 1964.

27. "Johnson Assails Goldwater View on Atomic Arms," *New York Times*, Aug. 16, 1964.

28. Barry Goldwater, *Goldwater* (New York: St. Martin's, 1988), 212.

29. Ibid., 213.

30. "GOP's Goldwater Busting Out All Over," *Newsweek*, May 20, 1963.

31. Perlstein, *Before the Storm*, 347.

32. Kathleen Hall Jamieson, *Packaging the Presidency: A History and Criticism of Presidential Campaign Advertising* (New York: Oxford, 1996), 205.

33. Benjamin C. Bradlee, *Conversations with Kennedy* (New York: W. W. Norton, 1984), 190.

34. "Text of Goldwater Speech on Rights," *New York Times*, June 19, 1964.

35. "Civil Rights Bill: 'It Will Not Be Denied,'" *Newsweek*, June 29, 1964.

36. Goldberg, *Barry Goldwater*, 189.

37. "At 8:25 p.m.: 'I'm Going to Run,'" *Newsweek*, June 22, 1964.

38. "The Fear and the Facts," *Time*, Sept. 25, 1964.

39. "At 8:25 p.m."

40. Goldberg, *Barry Goldwater*, 189; Jamieson, *Packaging the Presidency*, 179.

41. "Eisenhower Shift," *New York Times*, June 12, 1964; Goldberg, *Barry Goldwater*, 192–97; Perlstein, *Before the Storm*, 347.

42. "The New Thrust," *Time*, July 24, 1964; Jamieson, *Packaging the Presidency*, 183.

43. "The New Thrust"; Theodore H. White, *The Making of the President, 1964* (New York: Atheneum, 1965), 197, 201.

44. Lee Edwards, *The Conservative Revolution: The Movement That Remade America* (New York: Free Press, 1999), 83–84; 184–85.

45. Perlstein, *Before the Storm*, 27.

46. Kim Phillips-Fein, *Invisible Hands: The Making of the Conservative Movement from the New Deal to Reagan* (New York: W. W. Norton, 2009), 119–20.

47. Converse, Clausen, and Miller, "Electoral Myth and Reality," 321–36.

48. Gary Donaldson, *Liberalism's Last Hurrah: The Presidential Campaign of 1964* (Armonk, NY: M. E. Sharpe, 2003), 300.

49. Rovere, *The Goldwater Caper*, 41–42

50. Robert David Johnson, *All the Way with LBJ: The 1964 Presidential Election* (Cambridge: Cambridge University Press, 2009), 69.

51. Lyndon Johnson phone conversation with Robert Kennedy, July 21, 1964, WH 6407.12, #4299, www.whitehousetapes.net/tapes/johnson/telephone.

52. "Humphrey Warns of 'Twitchy' Hand on Nuclear Bomb," *New York Times*, Aug. 2, 1964.

53. Carl Solberg, *Hubert Humphrey: A Biography* (New York: W. W. Norton, 1984), 257–58.

54. John T. Woolley and Gerhard Peters, The American Presidency Project, Santa Barbara, CA, www.presidency.ucsb.edu/ws/?pid=26467.

55. White, *The Making of the President*, 315.

56. Jamieson, *Packaging the Presidency*, 169.

57. Goldwater, *Goldwater,* 198.

58. Survey by Louis Harris and Associates, Jan. 1964, from the iPOLL Databank, Roper Center for Public Opinion Research, University of Connecticut, www.ropercenter.uconn .edu/data_access/ipoll/ipoll.html.

59. Survey by Louis Harris and Associates, July 1964, iPOLL Databank.

60. Survey by Gallup Organization, Aug. 27–Sept. 1, 1964, iPOLL Databank.

61. Survey by Louis Harris and Associates, Sept. 1964, iPOLL Databank.

62. Johnson, *All the Way with LBJ,* 128.

63. Richard N. Goodwin, *Remembering America: A Voice from the Sixties* (New York: Harper and Row, 1988), 303.

64. Ibid., 303–4.

3. RULES ARE MADE TO BE BROKEN

1. David Kiley, *Getting the Bugs Out: The Rise, Fall and Comeback of Volkswagen in America* (New York: John Wiley, 2002), 86.

2. Rosser Reeves, *Reality in Advertising* (New York: Alfred A. Knopf, 1979), 46–49, 113.

3. David Ogilvy, *Confessions of an Advertising Man* (New York, Atheneum, 1963), 143.

4. Doris Willens, *Nobody's Perfect: Bill Bernbach and the Golden Age of Advertising* (n.p.: Create Space, 2009), 18.

5. Kenneth Roman, *The King of Madison Avenue: David Ogilvy and the Making of Modern Advertising* (New York: Palgrave Macmillan, 2009), 123.

6. Stephen Fox, *The Mirror Makers: A History of American Advertising and Its Creators* (Urbana: University of Illinois Press, 1997), 252.

7. Mark Tungate, *Adland: A Global History of Advertising* (London: Kogan Page, 2007), 48.

8. Thomas Frank, *The Conquest of Cool: Business Culture, Counterculture, and the Rise of Hip Consumerism* (Chicago: University of Chicago Press, 1997), 56.

9. Bob Levenson, *Bill Bernbach's Book: A History of the Advertising That Changed the History of Advertising* (New York: Villard, 1987), xvi.

10. Fox, *The Mirror Makers,* 255; Frank Rowsome, *Think Small: The Story of Those Volkswagen Ads* (Brattleboro, VT: Stephen Green Press, 1970), 86.

11. Jerry Della Femina, *From Those Wonderful Folks Who Gave You Pearl Harbor: Front-Line Dispatches from the Advertising War* (New York: Simon and Schuster, 1970), 154.

12. Author interview with Sidney Myers, Nov. 11, 2010.

13. Roman, *The King of Madison Avenue,* 124–26.

14. Willens, *Nobody's Perfect,* 31.

15. *Advertising Age,* "The Advertising Century," http://adage.com/century/campaigns .html.

16. Rowsome, *Think Small,* 69.

17. Ibid., 124.

18. Kiley, *Getting the Bugs Out,* 87.

19. Della Femina, *From Those Wonderful Folks Who Gave You Pearl Harbor,* 27.

20. Juliann Sivulka, *Soap, Sex, and Cigarettes: A Cultural History of American Advertising* (Belmont, CA: Wadsworth, 1998), 304–5.

21. Ibid., 307.

22. "When the Client Is a Candidate," *New York Times Magazine*, Oct. 25, 1964; Karl A. Lamb and Paul A. Smith, *Campaign Decision-Making: The Presidential Election of 1964* (Belmont, CA: Wadsworth, 1968), 159.

23. Records of the Democratic National Committee, Series II, Media Recommendation for the DNC 1964 Pres. Election, Folder: Pre-1964 correspondence with advertising agencies, Box 225, LBJ Library, Austin, Texas.

24. Lamb and Smith, *Campaign Decision-Making,* 159.

25. Kathleen Hall Jamieson, *Packaging the Presidency: A History and Criticism of Presidential Campaign Advertising,* 3rd ed. (New York: Oxford, 1996), 35.

26. "Advertising: Does It Have a Role in Politics?" *New York Times*, Oct. 27, 1963.

27. Jamieson, *Packaging the Presidency,* 85.

28. Gil Troy, *See How They Ran: The Changing Role of the Presidential Candidate* (New York: Free Press, 1991), 200.

29. Stanley Kelley, "Afterthoughts on Madison Avenue Politics," *Antioch Review* 17, no. 2 (Summer 1957): 173–86.

30. "Texts of Governor Stevenson's Speeches during His Invasion of Ohio," *New York Times*, Oct. 4, 1952.

31. Ball quoted in Beverly Merrill Kelley, *Reelpolitik: Political Ideologies in '50s and '60s Films,* vol. 2 (Lanham, MD: Rowman and Littlefield, 2004), 94.

32. Richard S. Salant, "The Television Debates: A Revolution That Deserves a Future," *Public Opinion Quarterly* 26, no. 3 (Autumn 1962): 342.

33. "Advertising: Does It Have a Role in Politics?" *New York Times*, Oct. 27, 1963.

34. Quoted in David B. Hill, "Political Campaigns and Madison Avenue: A Wavering Partnership," *Journal of Advertising* 13, no. 3 (1984); "Who's for Whom," *Time*, Sept. 11, 1964.

35. Joost A. M. Meerloo, *The Rape of the Mind: The Psychology of Thought Control, Menticide, and Brainwashing* (Cleveland: World Publishing, 1956), 97.

36. Gene Wyckoff, *The Image Candidates: American Politics in the Age of Television* (New York: Macmillan, 1968), 13.

37. G. Calvin Mackensie and Robert Weisbrot, *The Liberal Hour: Washington and the Politics of Change in the 1960s* (New York: Penguin, 2008), 36.

38. Shirley Vaughn Robson, "Advertising and Politics: A Case Study of the Relationship between Doyle Dane Bernbach, Inc., and the Democratic National Committee during the 1964 Presidential Campaign," M.A. thesis, American University, 1966.

39. Ibid., 5.

40. Ibid.

41. Author interview with Lloyd Wright, Sept. 2, 2010.

42. Robson, "Advertising and Politics"; Lamb and Smith, *Campaign Decision-Making,* 160.

43. "Advertising: The Political Campaign Trail," *New York Times*, Feb. 21, 1964; Lloyd Wright memo to Moyers et al., Mar. 11, 1964, Records of the Democratic National Committee, Series II, Doyle, Dane, and Bernbach, Folder: Doyle, Dane and Bernbach, Box 224, LBJ Library; author interview with Lloyd Wright, Sept. 2, 2010.

44. Jamieson, *Packaging the Presidency,* 173.

45. Wright interview with author, Sept. 2, 1010.

46. Lamb and Smith, *Campaign Decision-Making,* 195.

47. Lloyd Wright to Moyers et al., Mar. 25, 1964, Records of the Democratic National Committee, Series II, Doyle, Dane, and Bernbach, Folder: Doyle, Dane and Bernbach, Box 224, LBJ Library.

48. "Daisy: The Complete History of An Infamous and Iconic Ad," www.conelrad.com/daisy.

49. Author interview with Ann Barton, Apr. 1, 2009; Pete Hamill, "When the Client Is a Candidate," *New York Times Magazine,* Oct. 25, 1964.

50. Bernbach to Moyers, quoted in Jamieson, *Packaging the Presidency,* 173.

51. Hamill, "When the Client Is a Candidate."

52. "Daisy: The Complete History of An Infamous and Iconic Ad."

53. Hamill, "When the Client Is a Candidate."

4. THESE ARE THE STAKES

1. Gallup Poll conducted June 11–16, 1964, George H. Gallup, *The Gallup Poll: Public Opinion, 1935–1971,* vol. 3. (New York: Random House, 1972), 1890.

2. Lyndon Johnson phone conversation with George Reedy, July 20, 1964, WH 6407.11, #4286, www.whitehousetapes.net/tapes/johnson/telephone.

3. Bill Moyers e-mail message to author, Mar. 28, 2009.

4. George H. Gallup, *The Gallup Poll: Public Opinion, 1935–1971,* vol. 3 (New York: Random House, 1972), 1894.

5. Henry Wilson to Lawrence O'Brien, July 8, 1964, Papers of Lyndon B. Johnson, EX PL 3/17/64–4/30/63, Box 83, LBJ Library, Austin, Texas.

6. Norman Maher to Jack Valenti, July 20, 1964, Papers of Lyndon B. Johnson, White House Central Files, Aides: Office Files of Bill Moyers, Box 53, LBJ Library.

7. John Roche to Bill Moyers, June 12, 1964, Papers of Lyndon B. Johnson, White House Central Files, Aides: Office Files of Bill Moyers, Box 40, LBJ Library.

8. "The Woman Behind Barry Goldwater," *Good Housekeeping,* May 1964.

9. Lyndon Johnson phone conversation with Robert Kennedy, July 21, 1964, WH 6407.12, #4299, www.whitehousetapes.net/tapes/johnson/telephone.

10. Frank Cormier, *LBJ: The Way He Was* (Garden City, NY: Doubleday, 1977), 105.

11. Robert David Johnson, *All the Way with LBJ: The 1964 Presidential Election* (Cambridge: Cambridge University Press, 2009), 135.

12. Rick Perlstein, *Before the Storm: Barry Goldwater and the Unmaking of the American Consensus* (New York: Hill and Wang, 2001), 434

13. Richard N. Goodwin, *Remembering America: A Voice from the Sixties* (New York: Harper and Row, 1988), 304.

14. Pete Hamill, "When the Client Is a Candidate," *New York Times Magazine,* Oct. 25, 1964.

15. Shirley Vaughn Robson, "Advertising and Politics: A Case Study of the Relationship between Doyle Dane Bernbach, Inc., and the Democratic National Committee during the 1964 Presidential Campaign," M.A. thesis, American University, 1966; Hamill, "When

the Client Is a Candidate"; A. Petcavage to James Graham, May 21, 1964, Papers of Lyndon B. Johnson, White House Central Files, Aides: Office Files of Bill Moyers, Box 39, LBJ Library.

16. Robson, "Advertising and Politics."

17. G. Abraham to Bill Moyers, Aug. 6, 1964, Records of the Democratic National Committee, Series II, Doyle, Dane, and Bernbach, Box 224, LBJ Library.

18. DDB memo to Lloyd Wright and W. McCarthy, July 11, 1964, Records of the Democratic National Committee, Series II, Doyle, Dane, and Bernbach, Box 224, LBJ Library.

19. Robson, "Advertising and Politics"; Melvyn H. Bloom, *Public Relations and Presidential Campaigns: A Crisis in Democracy* (New York: Thomas Y. Crowell, 1973), 156.

20. DDB memo to Richard Goodwin et al., July 11, 1964, Records of the Democratic National Committee, Series II, Doyle, Dane, and Bernbach, Box 224, LBJ Library.

21. Goodwin, *Remembering America*, 304.

22. Sidney Myers quoted in: "Daisy: The Complete History of an Infamous and Iconic Ad," www.conelrad.com/daisy/daisy2.php.

23. Rowland Evans and Robert Novak, *Lyndon B. Johnson: The Exercise of Power* (New York: New American Library, 1966), 471–72.

24. William Bernbach to Bill Moyers, Aug. 17, 1964, Records of the Democratic National Committee, Series II, Doyle, Dane, and Bernbach, Box 224, LBJ Library.

25. Bill Moyers e-mail to author, March 28, 2009.

26. Harold Faber, ed., *The Road to the White House: The Story of the 1964 Election by the Staff of the New York Times* (New York: New York Times, 1965), 148–49.

27. "Johnson Assails Goldwater View on Atomic Arms," *New York Times*, Aug. 16, 1964.

28. Bill Moyers to Dick Maguire, Aug. 31, 1964, Records of the Democratic National Committee, Series II, Doyle, Dane, and Bernbach, Box 224, LBJ Library

29. DDB Script, "Confessions of a Republican," July 31, 1964, Records of the Democratic National Committee, Series II, Doyle, Dane, and Bernbach, Box 224, LBJ Library.

30. DDB memo from James Graham to William Bernbach et al., Aug. 4, 1964, Records of the Democratic National Committee, Series II, Doyle, Dane, and Bernbach, Box 224, LBJ Library.

31. DDB memo to Lloyd Wright, July 31, 1964, Records of the Democratic National Committee, Series II, Doyle, Dane, and Bernbach, Box 224, LBJ Library; "Daisy Girl" spot and transcript from The Living Room Candidate: Presidential Campaign Commercials, 1952–2008, Museum of the Moving Image, www.livingroomcandidate.org/commercials/1964.

32. "Tony Schwartz, Tape Master," *Audio,* Mar. 1994; Theodore H. White, *The Making of the President, 1964* (New York: Atheneum, 1965), xiv.

33. "Tony Schwartz, Father of 'Daisy Ad' for the Johnson Campaign, Dies at 84," *New York Times,* June 17, 2008; "Tony Schwartz: His Ads Targeted Viewer Emotions," *Washington Post,* June 17, 2008; "He's got Gotham on tape," *New York Daily News,* Sept. 3, 1999.

34. Audio of Polaroid and UN spots at www.conelrad.com/daisy/audio.php.

35. Myers quoted in "Daisy: The Complete History of an Infamous and Iconic Ad"; "Tony Schwartz, Tape Master," *Audio,* Mar. 1994; author interview with Sidney Myers, Nov. 18, 2010.

36. Schwartz quoted in Edwin Diamond and Stephen Bates, *The Spot: The Rise of Political Advertising on Television* (Cambridge, MA: MIT Press, 1988), 123.

37. Tony Schwartz, "My 'Daisy' Ad, and the G.O.P.'s," *New York Times,* Oct. 30, 2000.

38. Myers quoted in "Daisy: The Complete History of an Infamous and Iconic Ad"; author interview with Sidney Myers, Nov. 18, 2010.

39. Author interview with Sidney Myers, Nov. 18, 2010.

40. Ibid.; Myers and Geerhart quoted in "Daisy: The Complete History of an Infamous and Iconic Ad"; Aaron Ehrlich to Tony Schwartz, Jan. 17, 1991; James Graham to Peter Jennings, July 2, 1992, Sidney Myers to Leslie Wayne, Oct. 29, 2000, and Ann Barton to *New York Times,* Nov. 8, 2000, documents at: www.conelrad.com/daisy/documents.php

41. "When the Client Is a Candidate," *New York Times Magazine,* Oct. 25, 1964; "O'Brien and Aides Spark Party Hunt for Men, Funds," *Washington Post,* Sept. 29, 1968.

42. www.conelrad.com/daisy/video.php.

43. Bill Geerhart quoted in "Daisy: The Complete History of an Infamous and Iconic Ad."

44. "Daisy: The Complete History of an Infamous and Iconic Ad," www.conelrad.com/daisy/daisy2.php and http://conelrad.blogspot.com/2010/09/meet-real-daisy-girl-monique-corzilius.html; Richard Davenport-Hines, *Auden* (New York: Pantheon, 1999), 319; Edward Mendelson, *Later Auden* (New York: Farrar, 1999), 478; "Tony Schwartz, Tape Master"; author interview with Monique and Fred Corzilius, Nov. 11, 2010; author interview with Sidney Myers, Nov. 18, 2010; author interview with Colette Brunner, Jan. 20, 2011.

45. Paul Rutherford, *Endless Propaganda: The Advertising of Public Goods* (Toronto: University of Toronto Press, 2000), 31.

46. "Road to the White House," *Sponsor* 19 (Jan. 18, 1965).

47. Author interview with Lloyd Wright, Sept. 2, 2010.

48. Goodwin, *Remembering America,* 304–5. Lloyd Wright also recalled Moyers's words almost exactly as Goodwin recorded them (author interview with Lloyd Wright, Sept. 2, 2010).

49. DDB memo, James Graham to William Bernbach et al., Aug. 20, 1964, Records of the Democratic National Committee, Series II, Doyle, Dane, and Bernbach, Box 224, LBJ Library.

50. "Blanket Estimate for Budget Authorization," Aug. 24, 1964, Records of the Democratic National Committee, Series II, Doyle, Dane, and Bernbach, Box 224, LBJ Library; author interview with Sidney Myers, Nov. 18, 2010.

51. Hamill, "When the Client Is a Candidate."

5. THE HOMES OF AMERICA ARE HORRIFIED

1. Shirley Vaughn Robson, "Advertising and Politics: A Case Study of the Relationship between Doyle Dane Bernbach, Inc., and the Democratic National Committee during the 1964 Presidential Campaign," M.A. thesis, American University, 1966.

2. Author interview with Lloyd Wright, Sept. 2, 2010; Lloyd Wright e-mail to author, Oct. 4, 2010.

3. Lloyd Wright quoted in "Daisy: The Complete History of an Infamous and Iconic Ad," www.conelrad.com/daisy/daisy2.php.

4. Richard N. Goodwin, *Remembering America: A Voice from the Sixties* (New York: Harper and Row, 1988), 305.

5. Robson, "Advertising and Politics."

6. Drew Westin, *The Political Brain: The Role of Emotion in Deciding the Fate of the Nation* (New York: PublicAffairs, 2007), 56

7. "President Vows to Keep Control over Atom Arms," *New York Times*, July 8, 1964.

8. Author interview with Monique Luiz and Fred Corzilius, Nov. 11, 2010; author interview with Colette Brunner, Jan. 20, 2011.

9. Edwin Diamond and Stephen Bates, *The Spot: The Rise of Political Advertising on Television* (Cambridge, MA: MIT Press, 1988), 132; Merle Miller, *Lyndon: An Oral Biography* (New York: G. P. Putnam, 1980), 401.

10. Author interview with Lloyd Wright, Sept. 2, 2010; Bill Moyers e-mail to author, Mar. 28, 2009.

11. Jamieson, *Packaging the Presidency*, 200; author interview with Lloyd Wright, Sept. 2, 2010; see also, "The Fear and the Facts," *Time*, Sept. 25, 1964.

12. Diamond and Bates, *The Spot*, 132; Dean Burch to Charles Taft, Sept. 12, 1961, Papers of Charles P. Taft, I-26, Manuscript Division, Library of Congress (document also at www.conelrad.com/daisy/daisy_016.pdf); "Democratic TV 'Spot' Brings Formal Complaint by Burch," *Baltimore Sun*, Sept. 15, 1964.

13. Everett Dirksen to Vincent Washileski, Sept. 12, 1964, and Washileski to Dirksen, Sept. 15, 1964, White House Central Files, Aides: Office Files of Bill Moyers, LBJ Library, Austin, Texas; also at www.conelrad.com/daisy/daisy_021.pdf.

14. "'Unfair,' Cry GOP, Democrats at TV Efforts," *Advertising Age*, Sept. 21, 1964.

15. Author interview with Lloyd Wright, Sept. 2, 2010.

16. Jamieson, *Packaging the Presidency*, 200.

17. Transcript, "Meet the Press," Sept. 20, 1964, Records of the Democratic National Committee, Series I, Box 251, LBJ Library; Goodwin, *Remembering America*, 306.

18. Robert Albright, "Goldwater Stresses He's for Peace," *Winnipeg Free Press*, Nov. 2, 1964.

19. Barry Goldwater, *The Conscience of a Majority* (Englewood Cliffs, NJ: Prentice-Hall, 1970), 40–41.

20. Barry Goldwater, *Goldwater* (New York: St. Martin's Press, 1988), 254.

21. Moyers to Johnson, Sept. 13, 1964, Aides: Office Files of Bill Moyers, Box 53, LBJ Library; also at www.conelrad.com/daisy/daisy_017.pdf.

22. "G.O.P. Pledges Sane TV Ads for Campaign," *Chicago Tribune*, Sept. 14, 1964.

23. "New GOP Aide Blasts Democratic TV Short," *Washington Star*, October 6, 1964.

24. Karl Hess, *In a Cause That Will Triumph: The Goldwater Campaign and the Future of Conservatism* (Garden City, NY: Doubleday, 1967), 90.

25. Theodore H. White, *The Making of the President, 1964* (New York: Atheneum, 1965), 322.

26. "Political Ad Wheels Start to Turn—Slowly," *Advertising Age*, Sept. 7, 1964.

27. "Publicists Seek to Tie Barry to 'Extremists,' Show Cool, Busy LBJ," *Wall Street Journal*, Aug. 28, 1964.

28. White, *The Making of the President*, 321.

29. Ibid., 96.

30. Rush W. Dozier, *Fear Itself: The Origin and Nature of the Powerful Emotion That Shapes Our Lives and Our World* (New York: St. Martin's Press, 1998), 25.

31. Pete Hamill, "When the Client Is a Candidate," *New York Times Magazine*, Oct. 25, 1964.

32. Jack Valenti to Lyndon Johnson, Sept. 7, 1964, WHCF, EX PL 2, Box 84, LBJ Library.

33. Jack Valenti to Bill Moyers et al., Sept. 14, 1964, WHCF, EX PL 2, Box 84, LBJ Library.

34. Lloyd Wright to Bill Moyers, Sept. 14, 1964, WHCF, EX PL 2, Box 84, LBJ Library.

45. From The Living Room Candidate: Presidential Campaign Commercials, 1952–2008, Museum of the Moving Image, www.livingroomcandidate.org/commercials/1964.

36. Accessed at www.youtube.com/watch?v=4TJcD_RGecw; Jamieson, *Packaging the Presidency*, 201.

37. Jamieson, *Packaging the Presidency*, 202; author interview with Lloyd Wright, Sept. 2, 2010.

38. Susan A. Sherr, "Scenes from the Political Playground: An Analysis of the Symbolic Use of Children in Presidential Campaign Advertising," *Political Communication* 16:1 (1999): 45–59.

39. Jamieson, *Packaging the Presidency*, 202.

40. Rick Perlstein, *Before the Storm: Barry Goldwater and the Unmaking of the American Consensus* (New York: Hill and Wang, 2001), 432.

41. From The Living Room Candidate: Presidential Campaign Commercials, 1952–2008, Museum of the Moving Image, www.livingroomcandidate.org/commercials/1964.

42. Hayes Redmon to Bill Moyers, Sept. 18, 1964, Aides: Office Files of Bill Moyers, Box 53, LBJ Library.

43. John Bartlow Martin to Bill Moyers, Oct. 1, 1964, Aides: Office Files of Bill Moyers, Box 25, LBJ Library.

44. Lawrence O'Brien to Lyndon Johnson, Oct. 4, 1964, WHCF, EX PL 2, Box 84, LBJ Library.

45. Kenneth O'Donnell to Lyndon Johnson, Oct. 20, 1964, WHCF, EX PL 2, Box 85, LBJ Library.

46. Robson, "Advertising and Politics."

47. Arthur Krim oral history, June 29, 1982, LBJ Library.

48. Telephone recording of Lyndon Johnson–Willard Wirtz conversation, Oct. 5, 1965, WH 6410.03, #5838, Miller Center for Public Affairs, www.whitehousetapes.net/tapes/johnson/telephone.

49. Fred Dutton to Bill Moyers, Sept. 21, 1964, Aides: Office Files of Bill Moyers, Box 53, LBJ Library.

50. Murphy to Lyndon Johnson, Sept. 28, 1964, and Bill Moyers to Lyndon Johnson, Sept. 22, 1964, Aides: Office Files of Bill Moyers, Box 6, LBJ Library.

51. From The Living Room Candidate: Presidential Campaign Commercials, 1952–2008, Museum of the Moving Image, www.livingroomcandidate.org/commercials/1964.

52. Lyndon Johnson speech in Harrisburg, PA, Sept. 10, 1964, John T. Woolley and Gerhard Peters, The American Presidency Project, Santa Barbara, CA, www.presidency.ucsb.edu/ws/?pid=26494.

53. Lyndon Johnson speech in Texarkana, Feb. 25, 1964, Woolley and Peters, The American Presidency Project, www.presidency.ucsb.edu/ws/?pid=26530.

54. Lyndon Johnson speech at Johns Hopkins University, Oct. 1, 1964, Woolley and Peters, The American Presidency Project, www.presidency.ucsb.edu/ws/?pid=26546.

55. Lyndon Johnson speech at Alexandria, Virginia, Oct. 6, 1964, Woolley and Peters, The American Presidency Project, www.presidency.ucsb.edu/ws/?pid=26563.

56. Lyndon Johnson speech in Des Moines, Iowa, Oct. 7, 1964, Woolley and Peters, The American Presidency Project, www.presidency.ucsb.edu/ws/?pid=26570.

57. Lyndon Johnson speech text, Oct. 7, 1964, Woolley and Peters, The American Presidency Project, www.presidency.ucsb.edu/ws/?pid=26574.

58. Lyndon Johnson speech at South Gate, California, Oct. 11, 1964, Woolley and Peters, The American Presidency Project, www.presidency.ucsb.edu/ws/?pid=26588; Lyndon Johnson speech in Las Vegas, Oct. 11, 1964, Woolley and Peters, The American Presidency Project, www.presidency.ucsb.edu/ws/?pid=26590; Lyndon Johnson speech in Reno, Nevada, Oct. 12, 1964, Woolley and Peters, The American Presidency Project, www.presidency.ucsb.edu/ws/?pid=26593; Lyndon Johnson speech at New York City, Oct. 15, 1964, Woolley and Peters, The American Presidency Project, www.presidency.ucsb.edu/ws/?pid=26608; Lyndon Johnson speech at Orlando, Oct. 26, 1964, Woolley and Peters, The American Presidency Project, www.presidency.ucsb.edu/ws/?pid=26657.

59. Lyndon Johnson speech text, Nov. 2, 1964, Woolley and Peters, The American Presidency Project, www.presidency.ucsb.edu/ws/?pid=26714.

60. Robert Mann, *A Grand Delusion: America's Descent into Vietnam* (New York: Basic Books, 2001), 371–78

61. Robert David Johnson, *All the Way with LBJ: The 1964 Presidential Election* (Cambridge: Cambridge University Press, 2009), 245, 269.

62. Perlstein, *Before the Storm,* 427.

63. Ibid., 436.

64. White, *The Making of the President,* 349; Goodwin, *Remembering America,* 303; Perlstein, *Before the Storm,* 436–37; Rowland Evans and Robert Novak, *Lyndon B. Johnson: The Exercise of Power* (New York: New American Library, 1966), 468–69.

65. Bill Moyers to Lyndon Johnson, Sept. 29, 1964, WHCF, EX PL 2, Box 83, LBJ Library.

66. Goldwater, *Goldwater,* 210, 254.

67. Randall Bennett Woods, *LBJ: Architect of Ambition* (Cambridge: Harvard University Press, 2006), 550.

68. Exhibit 52, Sullivan Memoranda to John Dean, Jan. 31, 1975, Hearings by the Select Committee to Study Governmental Operations With Respect to Intelligence Activities of the United States Senate, 94th Congress, First Session, Vol. 6, Federal Bureau of Investigation, Nov. 18–19, 1975 and Dec. 2–3, 9–11, 1975, 539; Bill Moyers, "LBJ and the FBI," *Newsweek,* Mar. 10, 1975; Woods, *LBJ: Architect of Ambition,* 550. When asked by the author in 2010 about the details and propriety of the White House's request of the FBI, Moyers responded by forwarding the *Newsweek* article, observing, "I think it answers your questions" (e-mail from Moyers to author, Sept. 20, 2010).

69. Bill Moyers e-mail to author, March 28, 2009.

70. Author interview with Lloyd Wright, Sept. 2, 2010.

71. Bruce L. Felknor, *Dirty Politics* (New York: W. W. Norton, 1966), 235.

72. Hamill, "When the Client Is a Candidate."

73. Goodwin, *Remembering America,* 306.

74. Bill Moyers e-mail to author, Mar. 28, 2009; Goldwater, "Morality," from The Liv-

ing Room Candidate: Presidential Campaign Commercials, 1952–2008, Museum of the Moving Image, www.livingroomcandidate.org/commercials/1964/morality.

75. Bill Moyers e-mail to author, Mar. 28, 2009.

6. IN YOUR HEART, YOU KNOW HE MIGHT

1. Barry Goldwater, *Goldwater* (New York: St. Martin's, 1988), 252.

2. Theodore H. White, *The Making of the President, 1964* (New York: Atheneum, 1965), 329.

3. Kathleen Hall Jamieson, *Packaging the Presidency: A History and Criticism of Presidential Campaign Advertising* (New York: Oxford, 1996), 205.

4. "Goldwater Says 'We Are at War,'" *New York Times,* Sept. 20, 1964.

5. "Goldwater Says Generals Have a Nuclear Authority," *New York Times*, Sept. 23, 1964.

6. From The Living Room Candidate: Presidential Campaign Commercials, 1952–2008, Museum of the Moving Image, www.livingroomcandidate.org/commercials/1964/ike-at-gettysburg.

7. "Eisenhower on TV with Goldwater," *New York Times,* Sept. 23, 1964.

8. "Goldwater Lays War Aim to Reds," *New York Times*, Oct. 2, 1964.

9. White, *The Making of the President,* 325.

10. "Johnson Derides Goldwater View," *New York Times,* Oct. 25, 1964.

11. "The Fear and the Facts," *Time,* Sept. 25, 1964; see also "Our Defense: A Crucial Issue for Candidates," *Life,* Sept. 25, 1964.

12. Melvyn H. Bloom, *Public Relations and Presidential Campaigns: A Crisis in Democracy* (New York: Thomas Y. Crowell, 1973), 144–45.

13. Goldwater, *Goldwater,* 202.

14. Ibid., 198, 200.

15. Jamieson, *Packaging the Presidency,* 169.

16. White, *The Making of the President,* 357, 315.

17. "Those Outside Our Family," *Time,* July 24, 1964.

18. White, *The Making of the President,* 106–7.

19. "Kiddies, Here's a 'Guide to the Glories of LBJ,'" *Indianapolis Star,* Sept. 28, 1964.

20. Tony Schwartz, *The Responsive Chord* (New York: Anchor Press/Doubleday, 1973), 93–96.

21. "Politics and the Old Sales Pitch," *New York Times,* May 22, 1972.

22. From The Living Room Candidate: Presidential Campaign Commercials, 1952–2008, Museum of the Moving Image, www.livingroomcandidate.org/commercials/1964/peace-little-girl-daisy.

23. Tony Schwartz quoted in Edwin Diamond and Stephen Bates, *The Spot: The Rise of Political Advertising on Television,* rev. ed. (Cambridge, MA: MIT Press, 1988), 132.

24. Diamond and Bates, *The Spot,* 133.

25. Ralph Ginzburg, "Goldwater: The Man and the Menace," *Fact,* Sept.–Oct. 1964.

26. Warren Boroson, "What Psychiatrists Say about Goldwater," *Fact,* Sept.–Oct. 1964.

27. Richard E. Labunski, *Libel and the First Amendment: Legal History and Practice in Print and Broadcasting* (New Brunswick, NJ: Transaction, 1987), 123–24.

28. "Johnson's Wide Lead Reflects Confidence in Foreign Policy," *Washington Post,* Sept. 14, 1964.

29. "President Holds Lead of 2 to1 in Field of Inspiring Confidence," *Washington Post,* Oct. 26, 1964.

30. "Majority Sees Barry 'Nice Guy' of Courage, *Washington Post,* Oct. 30, 1964.

31. George H. Gallup, *The Gallup Poll: Public Opinion, 1935–1971,* vol. 3 (New York: Random House, 1972), 1906.

32. "Goldwater Cuts Johnson's Lead," *Washington Post,* Oct. 12, 1964.

33. "The Goldwater Threat," *Newsweek,* July 6, 1964.

34. "Who Said Barry Goldwater Was 'Impulsive'?" *New York Times,* July 12, 1964.

35. Jim Bishop, "His Lip Shoots from the Hip," *New York Journal-American,* July 29, 1964.

36. "300 Newspapers Backing Johnson," *New York Times,* Oct. 17, 1964.

37. "Comedians: The Campaign Jokes," *Time,* Sept. 18, 1964.

38. Quoted in "The Press: The Six-to-One Party Press," *Time,* Sept. 25, 1964; Karl E. Meyer, "The Unmaking of a Candidate," *New Statesman,* Sept. 19, 1964.

39. "Miami News for Johnson," *New York Times,* Sept. 22, 1964.

40. Rick Perlstein, *Before the Storm: Barry Goldwater and the Unmaking of the American Consensus* (New York: Hill and Wang, 2001), 426.

41. "Report to the Nation on Events in China and the USSR," Oct. 18, 1964, transcript at http://millercenter.org/scripps/archive/speeches/detail/5661.

42. "Johnson Hailed by 18,000 in Campaign Windup Here," *New York Times,* Nov. 1, 1964.

43. Dan Nimmo, *The Political Persuaders: The Techniques of Modern Election Campaigns* (Englewood Cliffs, NJ: Prentice-Hall, 1970), 134.

44. "Choice," 1964, International Historic Films, #22950; Joanne Morreale, *The Presidential Campaign Film: A Critical History* (Westport, CT: Praeger, 1993), 70–75; from "Conelrad Adjacent," http://conelrad.blogspot.com/2010/10/choice-1964-story-conference.html; John William Middendorf, *A Glorious Disaster: Barry Goldwater and the Origins of the Conservative Movement* (New York: Basic Books, 2006), 203.

45. "Choice."

46. "Conelrad Adjacent"; Morreale, *The Presidential Campaign Film;* Middendorf, *A Glorious Disaster.*

47. From The Living Room Candidate: Presidential Campaign Commercials, 1952–2008, Museum of the Moving Image, www.livingroomcandidate.org/commercials/1964/morality.

48. From The Living Room Candidate: Presidential Campaign Commercials, 1952–2008, Museum of the Moving Image, www.livingroomcandidate.org/commercials/1964/ronald-reagan.

49. Steven F. Hayward, *The Age of Reagan: The Fall of the Old Liberal Order, 1964–1980* (New York: Random House, 2009), x–xi.

50. "He Speaks for Courage," paid advertisement, *Los Angeles Times,* Nov. 1, 1964.

51. Stanley Kelley, "The Presidential Campaign," in *The National Election of 1964,* ed.

Milton C. Cummings Jr. (Washington: Brookings Institution, 1966), 61.

52. White, *The Making of the President,* 300.

53. Middendorf, *A Glorious Disaster,* 213.

54. John Bartlow Martin, "Election of 1964," in *History of American Presidential Elections, 1789–1968,* vol. 4, ed. Arthur M. Schlesinger Jr. (New York: McGraw-Hill, 1971), 3594.

55. George H. Gallup, *The Gallup Poll: Public Opinion, 1935–1971,* vol. 3 (New York: Random House, 1972), 1868, 1900, 1904; Gallup Poll (AIPO), Jan. 1964 and Aug. 1964, from the iPOLL Databank, Roper Center for Public Opinion Research, University of Connecticut, www.ropercenter.uconn.edu/data_access/ipoll/ipoll.html.

56. "Hopes and Fears" survey, Gallup Poll, Sept. 1964, iPOLL Databank.

57. "Hopes and Fears," Gallup Poll, Oct. 1964, iPOLL Databank.

58. Ibid.

59. Harris Survey, Oct. 1964, iPOLL Databank.

60. Gallup polls, Dec.1963–Oct. 1964 (AIPO), iPOLL Databank; Harris Survey polls were published in the *Washington Post* throughout 1964.

61. "Electoral Myth and Reality: The 1964 Election," Philip E. Converse, Aage R. Clausen, and Warren E. Miller, eds. *American Political Science Review* 59, no. 2 (June 1965): 321–36.

62. Gallup Poll (AIPO), Nov. 1964, iPOLL Databank.

63. "Hopes And Fears," Gallup Poll, Oct. 1964, iPOLL Databank.

64. "Electoral Myth and Reality."

CONCLUSION

1. Theodore H. White, *The Making of the President, 1960* (New York: Atheneum, 1961), 110–12.

2. Edwin Diamond and Stephen Bates, *The Spot: The Rise of Political Advertising on Television* (Cambridge, MA: MIT Press, 1992), 57–58.

3. "Sills Family," Democratic National Committee, 1960, from The Living Room Candidate: Presidential Campaign Commercials, 1952–2008, Museum of the Moving Image, www.livingroomcandidate.org/commercials/1960/sills-family.

4. "Jingle," Citizens for Kennedy-Johnson, 1960, video courtesy of the John F. Kennedy Presidential Library, from The Living Room Candidate: Presidential Campaign Commercials, 1952–2008, Museum of the Moving Image, www.livingroomcandidate.org/commercials/1960/jingle.

5. From The Living Room Candidate: Presidential Campaign Commercials, 1952–2008, Museum of the Moving Image, www.livingroomcandidate.org/commercials/1960.

6. "Mother and Child," and "Bomb (Nuclear Treaty)," Citizens for Humphrey-Muskie, 1968, maker: Tony Schwartz, video courtesy of the Minnesota Historical Society, from The Living Room Candidate: Presidential Campaign Commercials, 1952–2008, from Museum of the Moving Image, www.livingroomcandidate.org/commercials/1968/mother-and-child and www.livingroomcandidate.org/commercials/1968/bomb-nuclear-treaty.

7. "Child's Face," Nixon, 1968, makers: Leonard Garment, Harry Treleaven, Frank Shakespeare, and Eugene Jones, video courtesy of the Nixon Presidential Library and Mu-

seum, from The Living Room Candidate: Presidential Campaign Commercials, 1952–2008, Museum of the Moving Image, www.livingroomcandidate.org/commercials/1968/childs-face.

8. Joe McGinniss, *The Selling of the President* (New York: Penguin, 1969), 172, 187–89.

9. Ibid., 191–94.

10. Kathleen Hall Jamieson, *Packaging the President: A History and Criticism of Presidential Campaign Advertising* (New York: Oxford, 1996), 227; Tony Schwartz, *The Responsive Chord* (New York: Anchor Press/Doubleday, 1973), 92–93.

11. Ibid., 81–82.

12. Ibid., 96.

13. Robert Edmonds Kintner, *Broadcasting and the News* (New York: Harper and Row, 1965).

14. Joanne Morreale, *The Presidential Campaign Film: A Critical History* (Westport, CT: Praeger, 1993), 70.

15. The Living Room Candidate: Presidential Campaign Commercials, 1952–2008, Museum of the Moving Image, www.livingroomcandidate.org/commercials/1984/bear and www.livingroomcandidate.org/commercials/1988/revolving-door.

16. Paul Rutherford, *Endless Propaganda: The Advertising of Public Goods* (Toronto: University of Toronto Press, 2000), 32.

17. Annette Simmons, *The Story Factor: Inspiration, Influence, and Persuasion through the Art of Storytelling,* 2nd rev. ed. (New York: Basic Books, 2006), 51.

18. Schwartz, *The Responsive Chord*, 93.

19. Barry Goldwater, *Goldwater* (New York: St. Martin's, 1988), 252.

20. Scott Jacobs, "Nonfallacious Rhetorical Strategies: Lyndon Johnson's Daisy Ad," *Argumentation* 20, no. 4 (Dec. 2006), 434.

21. Neil Postman, *Amusing Ourselves to Death: Public Discourse in the Age of Show Business* (New York: Penguin, 1985), 50.

22. "Who Said Barry Goldwater Was 'Impulsive'?" *New York Times,* July 12, 1964.

23. Goldwater, *Goldwater,* 254–55.

24. Robert Spero, *The Duping of the American Voter: Dishonesty and Deception in Presidential Television Advertising* (New York: Lippincott and Crowell, 1980), 82.

25. David Broder, "And What about a Hitler," in *The Political Image Merchants: Strategies in the New Politics,* ed. Ray Eldon Hiebert et al. (Washington: Acropolis Books, 1971), 22.

26. John G. Geer, *In Defense of Negativity: Attack Ads in Presidential Campaigns* (Chicago: University of Chicago Press, 2006), 3.

27. Jacobs, "Nonfallacious Rhetorical Strategies," 436.

INDEX